Dialectics

By the Same Author

- *An Integrated Science of the Absolute*
- *Saundaryalaharī* (Commentary)
- *The Bhagavad Gita* (Commentary)
- *The Autobiography of an Absolutist*
- *The Word of the Guru*
- *Experiencing One World*
- *Unitive Philosophy*
- *One Hundred Verses of Self Instruction* (Commentary)
- *Wisdom*

Dialectics

Nataraja Guru

PRINTWORLD
Publishers of Indian Traditions

Cataloging in Publication Data – DK

[Courtesy: D.K. Agencies (P) Ltd. <docinfo@dkagencies.com>]

Nataraja Guru, 1895-1973, **author.**
Dialectics / Nataraja Guru.
pages cm
Reprint of: Third edition, 2010.
Includes bibliographical references and index.
ISBN 9788124604441 (PB)
1. Dialectic. 2. Dialectical materialism – Methodology.
I. Title.

LCC B809.8.N38 2025 | DDC 146.32 23

ISBN: 978-81-246-0444-1
First edition published in 1977
Second edition published in 1993
Third edition published in 2010
Reprinted in 2017, 2025

Author: Nataraja Guru (1895-1973)

Printed and published by:
D.K. Printworld (P) Ltd.
Regd. office: "Vedaśrī", F-395, Sudarshan Park
(Metro Station: ESI Hospital), New Delhi - 110015
Phones: (011) 4172 2626, 98713 94815
e-mail: indology@dkprintworld.com
Website: www.dkprintworld.com

Foreword to the Second Edition

THIS book was originally published under the title *Dialectical Methodology*. The central theme of this book is dialectics. The several shades of Yoga that are possible between man and woman come under the purview of "Man-Woman Dialectics." The great writers of all time have written their absorbing poems, epics, dramas, novels, short stories and psychological treatises based on this subject.

Freud says, sex is the hub on which all human interests revolve. We find an identical verse given by Narayana Guru, in the *Ātmopadeśa Śatakam* (One Hundred Verses of Self-Instruction) Verse 70:

> One *rati* alone expands into the ego, the senses,
> The mind, the body and all that is;
> Where is an end to this?
> As long as one knows that the knower is different;
> remember!

This book of Nataraja Guru is a long-awaited one. The Narayana Gurukula is republishing it. Hope this will be a welcome addition to the ever-increasing Guru-literature.

Fernhill,
17-9-1993

Nitya Chaitanya Yati

The unreal cannot have becoming,
And the real cannot exist without becoming;
The inner secret in respect of the two
Is seen only by a real seer.

— Bhagavad Gita II.4

Foreword to the First Edition

It is generally believed that dialectical methodology originated in the West in the fifth century BCE with Zeno of Elea. What Zeno used as an argument with paradoxes for philosophical purposes thereafter degenerated in the hands of the Sophists. Although Protagoras was a Sophist, it is believed (his works are no longer available) that he gave a precise methodological validity to dialectics. Socrates used dialectics as an art of discussion. However, according to Aristotle, the Socratic method was not dialectical. He called it *epagogic*, meaning inductive reasoning.

Dialectical methodology, lost in the hands of the Sophists, was revived and made thoroughly efficient by Plato in his *Dialogues*. He considered dialectics as a supreme philosophical method and even glorified it as "the coping stone, as it were, placed above the sciences." In Books VI and VII of the *Republic*, Plato even designated it as the right kind of education to be given to philosopher kings.

Aristotle considered dialectics as a logic of probability. He evaluated it as a useful discipline for intellectual training, for discussions with others based on their own premises, and for examining the unprovable first principles of the sciences.

Among Christian theologians of scholastic times one who gave serious attention to dialectics was Peter Abelard. In his *Dialectica* he offered a complete methodological treatment of the method of dialectics.

Of the modern philosophers, it was Kant who brought dialectics back to an honoured position as a philosophical methodology. In his *Critique of Pure Reason* he presented his theory of transcendental dialectics with four sets of theses and antitheses. However, he did not postulate synthesis to go along with thesis and antithesis. He used synthetical judgment a priori in the context of mathematical reasoning.

It was Fichte who introduced for the first time the famous dialectical triad of thesis, antithesis and synthesis. Although many people associate this triad with Hegelian dàilectics, he did not actually use these terms. Yet all credit should be given to Hegel for showing the vast scope of dialectics when it is used to interpret history and to understand the socio-psychological phenomena of human behaviour.

Karl Marx borrowed from Fichte the dialectical interplay of thesis and antithesis resulting in synthesis, and used it as his main instrument to probe and study the socio-economic reality of contemporary history. He saw in dialectics, as did Hegel, a progressive spiralling that leads the history of human evolution from one synthesis to another synthesis. As his identity was with the proletarian cause, he did not appreciate the continued progress of the dialectical spiral beyond the withering of the State. His associate, Friedrich Engels, enlarged the scope of dialectics in *The Dialectics of Nature*.

When Nataraja Guru uses the term Dialectical Methodology, he has in mind a hoary tradition of the East, well known to Indian scholars as Yoga Mīmāṁsā, as well as his understanding of the application of dialectics in the West. Dialectics is taken for granted as an implicit method in all the Upanishads. Mımamsa means "critical enquiry" and Yoga means "effecting synthesis." Both the schools of Pūrva Mīmāṁsā and Uttara Mīmāṁsā have adopted critical enquiry as part of their discipline. Dialectics as a critique of unitive understanding is most effectively used in the Bhagavad Gita and the *Yoga-Vāsiṣṭha*. In the philosophical writings of Nataraja Guru, we get an integrated vision of the East and the West, the past and the present. He has evolved an overall scheme of correlation in which the *catuṣpāda*, the four-limbed scheme of the Absolute of the *Mandukya Upanishad*, and the Cartesian coordinates are fused into a single frame of reference. Guru's main contribution to philosophy is this unitive understanding and, for the presentation of it, he uses the comprehensive methodology of dialectics.

In the present book, the Guru not only elucidates the dialectical methodology as such, but also applies it to the relationship between man and woman, proto-language and meta-language (associated with Indian iconography), which comes under the section of "The Dialectics of the Gods," and romance and tragedy in literature. Nataraja Guru applies dialectics to the study of social problems as was previously done by Hegel, Marx and Engels. However, in his application of dialectics to social problems, he is at variance with these philosophers. In that field he is more at ease with J.J. Rousseau and Henri Bergson.

All the sections in the present book were formerly published in *Values* magazine between May 1958 and October 1960, and we are very happy to republish the same now in the present book form. It is our cherished hope that we will be able to bring out all the written works of Nataraja Guru in the course of the next couple of years. We hope this book will benefit all those who want to have an insight into unitive understanding in general and particularly into the teachings of Nataraja Guru's own master, Narayana Guru.

Nitya Chaitanya Yati

East-West University
of Brahmavidya
Sreenivasapuram, Varkala
December 26, 1977

Contents

When a person starts on the discovery of the Absolute by the light of the reason only, without the assistance of the senses, and never desists until by pure intelligence he arrives at the perception of the Absolute Good, he at last finds himself at the end of the intellectual world. . . .

Dialectics then is the coping stone of the sciences, and is set over them; it would not be right to place any other science higher, the nature of knowledge cannot further go.

— Plato

1

Dialectical Methodology

From "Bread" as a fundamental necessity to "Freedom" with the capital letter, is the amplitude of human concern within whose range the inner being of man ever oscillates alternately. Man is ever engaged in matching means with ends, small or great, near or far, involving shorter or longer spans of interest. When ends and means tally, he is satisfied and happy.

There is a whole hierarchy of interests natural to man. The stage of life and the type of person according to variations of mood or the unravelling of instincts, give room for many varieties of satisfaction possible in human life, when ends and means are brought together through intelligence.

Methodology emerges when orderliness is attempted in this constant task of matching ends and means, of which life mainly consists. Dialectical methodology is that crowning approach to life's problems, independently of outside things or objects, and whereby satisfactions take place through the matching of means with ends or vice versa, within pure consciousness itself.

Dialectics has been called (by Plato) the coping stone of wisdom, and the dialectical method is the exercise of a faculty which is the precious privilege and heritage which distinguishes man. Although known and used by great minds throughout the ages, it is a method that has still to be positively formulated in unitive and universal terms, free from parochialisms and closed orthodoxies. The mystery of the dialectical way has once again to be stated in broad daylight, so that modern civilization may be saved from lopsided or one-legged progression, as at present. What is still available in disjunct regions, in distinct traditions of wisdom, has to be restated in universally open, dynamic and revalued terms through the clarification of the methodology which alone would apply to the highest aspiration of man, namely, the attainment of the Absolute.

Varieties of Method Used Hitherto

From simple trial and error methods leading to the measurements and experiments of the physical sciences, and to the methods of pure mathematics, where axiomatic verities are examined and interpreted through hypothesis and deduction, we have a whole range of methods suited for different branches of science or reasoning. Inductive and deductive inferences alternate with ones which are a priori and a posteriori. The general and the particular lend degrees of certitude to one another.

By muddling through a combination of hypothesis and fact, the physical world which is man's habitat, has been interpreted according to the intelligent notions of thinkers from the time of Pythagoras to Eddington. Newton's universe is not the same as that of Einstein. The geological age of the earth is different from that of the thermodynamical. This is because the methods used, the norms selected and the scope of the particular branch of knowledge of the scientists themselves vary. The methodology is adapted to suit the requirements and objects of each.

There is at present no unified methodology common to all the sciences. When statistical, historical, descriptive and psychological methods are all admitted as valid, and when questionnaires are relied upon to arrive at certitudes, what passes for scientific method in general has at present no common basis or universal validity. Even in arriving at a correct notion of the empirical world, much of what passes for method is really not different from a glorified form of guesswork.

If we leave behind such human ambitions as the conquests of outer space, where a unified methodology seems least to apply, and come to more theoretical fields such as matching action with reaction, cause with its effect, in order to live more intelligently in a utilitarian world, thinking of the greatest good of the greatest number, we come to what we might call the ratiocinative methodology by which ends and means are brought together, though dualistically. According to J.S. Mill there are five ways of studying cause and effect relations, namely: by agreement, by difference, by both these together, by concomitant variations, and by residue. What is interesting here is to note that both cause and effect are given an equal status and brought together so that one might suggest the other and help to bridge the gap between ends and means in our life where many utilitarian problems have to be solved. The dialectical method is only foreshadowed here.

Purer Methods of Rationalism and Idealism

If we follow still further the development of method into the higher domain of non-utilitarian thought, we come to philosophers such as Descartes, Spinoza and Kant. Maxims like *cogito ergo sum* (I think, therefore I am), and the possibility of a priori reasoning which was Kant's characteristic, may be seen to belong to a world of purer reason where inner values become realities by their own right.

The body-mind duality of Descartes and the difference between "pure" and "practical" reasons in Kant left the unitive Absolute untouched, and to this extent their methodology was not fully dialectical. In Spinoza, however, who thought in terms of a central "substance" that has an absolute status, we come very near to a form of reasoning which serves the same purpose as that of a fully dialectical method. The method of Hegel which claimed to be based on dialectics, can be credited to be dialectical only to the extent that the counterparts of a given historical situation were treated unitively by him with the names of thesis, antithesis and synthesis applied to them.

This dialectical way of reasoning with a historical bias is a brand of dialectical method which is very partial in its scope and application. Pre-Socratic philosophers like Zeno and Parmenides employed the fully dialectical method to certain problems such as the big and the small, and the one and the many, in a purer form. Much wider, however, in its scope and application, is the dialectical methodology as used in such books as the Bhagavad Gita and as implied in many parts of the Upanishads. When the Absolute is the subject matter, the scope of this method attains to its fullest development in human thought.

Thus from the trial and error method known to the empirical sciences, where *either* a generic *or* a specific verity counts at a given moment, we gradually pass on through intermediate stages of the development of methods in thinking, where ratiocination yields place to pure reasoning; and soon we pass further on to idealistic thought where dialectical counterparts emerge in the thesis and the antithesis which resolve themselves into the unitive terms of the synthesis. We find that even at this last stage vestiges of duality as between ends and means persist. When action and reaction, cause and effect, ends and means, come together unitively round a central reality that has an Absolute status, then dialectical methodology may be said to have come to its own.

The Marks of Dialectical Methodology Proper

A methodology still tainted or vitiated by expressions such as "but," "if," or "either-or" may be said to be hesitant or faltering in its approach to Verity or Value. These are terms man uses when he does not know what he wants.

When epistemological duality has been abolished in thinking, and when wholehearted or one-pointed interest which is legitimate and natural to man is initiated in his attitude, he begins to speak in terms of a greater certitude. An affiliation to or initiation into dialectical methodology may be said to take place when the "either-or" mentality or attitude of lukewarm compromise gives way to a more radical and one-pointed interest in the end within his means in a given case. The target and the arrow have to fall into a unitive agreement. Right means and right ends would then justify both together, and the mean where major and minor terms meet with equal and reciprocal status would represent the goal of wisdom.

The expression *api-ca* (also too) which repeats itself in such dialectically conceived texts as the Bhagavad Gita so profusely (at least two hundred times), is a clear indication of the dialectical methodology employed by its author. This same methodology is twice referred to with different normative concepts in the *Īśa Upanishad* where the pair of values called *vidyā* (knowledge) and *avidyā* (nescience), and the pair of values called *sambhūti* (becoming) and *vināśa* (destruction), one pair that is psychological and the other cosmological in content, are unitively revalued according to a dialectical method that was once consciously employed by Indian thinkers and afterwards lapsed into disuse. Similarly, when cause and effect, father and son relationship, or master and servant relationship are taken, they can be dialectically treated or unilaterally treated in a one-legged or lame fashion. The father and son relationship, unitively conceived, should not slant even a little on the side of one or the other. The son's father and the father's son should refer to one and the same human value or regulating principle in human life. The verity that is thus neutral and central between two terms of reciprocal propositions may be said to represent the Absolute, norm of that context, in the light of the dialectical method dealt with here.

The Absolute is not a Thing

The Absolute is not a thing, a meaning, or even an "ism" exclusive of others. The methodology of such a reality is indifferent to the stimulant words which, whatever context it might belong to, can evoke the normative principle proper to science.

As a set of cooking pots of different sizes but of the same shape can be serially fitted into one another, like the sections of a portable telescope, the larger of the series having the same centre of gravity as the smaller, so in dialectical methodology, all worlds or values in outer or inner life can be unitively treated with no reference to outer specific attributes. Thus it is that Vedanta can include all previous *darśana*s (points of philosophic view) and regard them as dialectical revaluations of the same Absolute principle.

Each *darśana* or system is free to have its own central norm to which it can give primacy for the time being, without hurting or affecting the absolutist content which remains the same anyway. The Upanishads thus place "Food" in the central position as representing the Absolute sometimes, and at other times the "Word" that is neutral between a guru (teacher) and a *śiṣya* (disciple) is put as the Absolute Norm at the centre of another way of approaching the Absolute through dialectical methodology.

A wholehearted bipolar relation as between subject and object, the seer and the seen, knowledge and known, is all that is required to be established to justify the use of dialectical methodology in respect of the unitive and neutral value implicit in that relationship. Thus a wife could treat her husband (or vice versa) as the representative of the adorable Value or the Absolute and attain to supreme felicity which is in principle no other than the ultimate term of spiritual life. The unconditioned happiness that results is proof of the final or ultimate character of the value involved, which is independent of both husband and wife at the same time.

Even attachment to an inanimate object, when established in correct compliance with the principles of dialectical methodology and as referring to the Absolute, would serve the same purpose. From a wooden or stone stump to the cosmic principle, all grades of reality can be viewed unitively as the same, from inside as it were, without violating the tenets of dialectical methodology. Thus it is that each chapter of the Bhagavad Gita takes a different human value-factor to serve in its discussion of the Absolute, while still retaining its strict unity and universality of subject and treatment. Pantheism, eclecticism, solipsism, syncretism, nominalism, monism, and conceptualism become, thus viewed, only corollaries or aspects of dialectical methodology as applied to the Absolute, which is reality in its perfect totality.

The Initial Affiliative Step

Though not in a theological or mystical sense, one has to be "initiated" into the way of dialectical reasoning. The changeover from a Newtonian or Euclidean world to that, say, of Einstein or Eddington takes long years of soaking into the epistemology, methodology and value factors that hang together giving unity to them. The notion of the Absolute, which we have said is the *end*, which has to be unitively understood with the *means* thereof, has many particularities and peculiarities which take some time to sink into the consciousness. A person lost in the middle of a large city which is new to him and with only confused directions, would take some time to orientate himself correctly.

The rational, cogitative, meditative and contemplative approaches to philosophical problems may again vary. The dualist methodology of the empiricists might also change complexion gradually as we ascend from the ontological, supporting ourselves through mechanistic, Aristotelian logic, or, more truly dialectical reasoning, through the successive levels of existence or subsistence or value. Even the matter of riding a bicycle cannot be taught by one or even a few instructions. Using force on the pedals has to alternate, and the balance has to be kept depending on which way the bicycle slants or where the pedal concerned has arrived in its revolution. If a simple matter such as this takes experience and sympathetic understanding of a number of factors that hang together, it should not be difficult to concede that the Science of the Absolute requires personal guidance and initiation.

A bipolar rapport or sympathy has to be established between the teacher of wisdom and the student so that the wisdom baby may safely see the light of day. Although the giving birth to wisdom can be one's own, at least the midwife's role in the affair is that of a guru who initiates. In some rare cases Nature itself and God as a vague invisible factor, may serve the role of such a guru. All we want to indicate here is that when ends and means have to be unitively treated in dialectical methodology, it also follows, at least as a corollary of the same, that the teacher and the taught have to enter into what may be called a unitive pact so that through a sort of osmosis, as it were, dialectical wisdom may flow normally from one person to the other. Guruhood and initiation are thus part and parcel of dialectical methodology. The Self and the non-Self are related here.

Dialectics Unconsciously Implied in All Philosophizing

Dialectics, no more than philosophizing, cannot operate in a vacuum. If the Absolute, could be existent and non-existent at once, the method that leads to such a notion has, for the sake of argument at least, to postulate a process called knowing which can take place within a split second or within eternal duration.

All speculative philosophies in the whole world have epistemological, methodological or value notions hanging together and connected with some sort of explicit or implicit process of knowing or emancipation. Being and becoming treated together would admit of the normal employment of a method. Different branches of philosophy or their schools, in their speculations, invariably employ paired expressions which recur as twins again and again in the literature proper of the particular school. Ontology and teleology, the necessary and the contingent, the immanent and the transcendent, the subjective and the objective, the practical and the pure, the phenomenon and the noumenon, are paired expressions without which no philosopher can outshine another. These expressions are seen further to have a subtle reciprocity, interdependence, polarity, antinomy or ambivalence between them.

If we turn again to the Indian scene of philosophical speculation, we find expressions such as *jñāna* (wisdom) and *karma* (action), *sāmānya* (generic) and *viśeṣa* (specific), *sādhana* (means) and *sādhya* (ends), *parā* (transcendent) and *aparā* (immanent), which refer to the dichotomous or dual aspects of the Absolute. To reduce *bheda* (difference) into *abheda* (non-difference) is the aim of Advaita (non-duality). The *jīva* (life principle) here and the *brahman* (cosmic principle) there have to be equated, or, in the merely cosmological context, the *pindānda* (microcosm) has to be related to the *brahmānda* (macrocosm).

Such is the course of speculation whether in the East or the West. Dialectical methodology proper has the task of matching these pairs of concepts into one system which is globally and universally conceived, instead of in piecemeal, haphazard or closed relativistic fashion as at present.

The Ascent and Descent Involved

When in common parlance it is even now stated that the Absolute is perfect or that God is absolute, being omnipresent, omniscient and omnipotent, the essence of dialectical methodology is already tacitly admitted.

If God created all, then what about the evil? If God is omnipresent, then, is he not present in hell too? If God is omniscient, does he not know the workings of Satan? If God is omnipotent, does he not connive at Satan's work? These are some of the corollaries which could be derived from the absolute attributes of God, which popular theology might fight shy of and try to evade. The bolder dialectical stand takes a more unitive view in which good and evil cancel out in the perfection of the Absolute. In fact, in the Arian controversy, the consubstantiality of the Father, Son and Holy Ghost was a doctrine that could never be settled except by the intervention of the Pagan Emperor Constantine who forced the doctrine on the Catholic Church. On that day dialectics may be said to have been tacitly, though not openly, accepted by the orthodox churches. The converse phenomenon of the ascension of the Christ refers to a doctrine which is similar in its content. Theology readily accepts an ascent and a descent in the closed world of contemplative values. The Pagan Mysteries held this secret as their own, much anterior to its hesitant acceptance in the world of scholastic and patristic theology. The Hermetics had the dictum that what was above was also here below, and the Upanishadic *mantra* (incantation) *pūrṇam adaḥ pūrṇam idam* (plenitude there and plenitude here) has the same principle of dialectical ascent and descent implied. *Paradise Lost* and *Paradise Regained* is based on the same movement as in Dante's *Divine Comedy*. The Bhagavad Gita and the philosophy of Plotinus contain elements of these twin movements scrutinized more microscopically into its mechanism. This dialectical way is therefore one of great antiquity and universality. The archetypal pattern of human thought itself may be said to contain this subtle secret at its core.

Even modern speculation has not got totally rid of this pattern, and herein is a hope for modern thought to be able to catch up once more with this way which has been conserved by the best of philosophers through successive generations through millennia, and still surviving today as the secret of the popular teachers in disjunct corners of the world. In his report published in the *Annurre du College de France*, Paris for the year 1948, Prof. Louis Lavelle, summarizing his course during the year, states:

> Finally the question poses itself as to how the unity of the spirit could engender the multiplicity of ideas; and if it is possible for one to ascend from the world to the world of ideas by way of an ascending dialectic, it is descending dialectic which is the proper object of metaphysics. . . .
>
> Already in the days of antiquity Aristotle had made Platonic thought take a decisive step forward by substituting for the opposition of the two worlds (of ideas and of things) of which one is a changeless model of the other, the conversion of power

> into action which realized itself at the core of the individual in such a manner that, while for Aristotle primarily it was a question of showing how the idea incarnated itself, for Plato it was a question of showing, on the contrary, how it disincarnated.[1]

Marxist Type of Materialist Dialectics

In order to clarify the application of the dialectical method in a living situation which is available for us to study, we have the example of the Marxist school of philosophers who avowedly employ the dialectical method.

Three eminent spokesmen of this school which holds much topical interest in contemporary thought, have taken special care to explain before the Indian Philosophical Congress held at Srinagar, Kashmir, 1957, that it would be completely wrong to mix up the materialism of Marx with mere materialism or even with pragmatism as understood in America, which, one of these Russians said, was akin to the philosophy of selfish profit-making. Prof. A. Shishkin of the Institute of Philosophy, Moscow, stated categorically:

> Dialectics and historical materialism serves as the philosophic foundation of the Marxist theory of social revolution. Does this statement mean that the Marxist materialism pays all attention to the material side of society and rejects the necessity and importance of the human ideals, the necessity and importance of the high development of the human mind and human emotions?
>
> But it is not so in the least. Marxism does not deny the importance of ideals. . . . Marxism does not put aside the task of spiritual and moral renovation of man.[2]

Prof. P.V. Kopnin of the same Institute used more enigmatic language apropos the relation between thought and action. In

1. p. 121 translated.
2. Proceedings, pp. 185-86.

using the more correct and balanced dialectical method to correlate these two counterparts in human life, the eminent professor stated:

> The criterion of practice is both absolute and relative. It is absolute because it proves the objective truth of thought. . . . It is relative because at a certain definite stage of history it is incapable of fully confirming or disproving all the existing theoretical construction. . . . Therefore it is only in the process of its own development that practice may serve as a criterion for the truth of a developing thought.[3]

What we can roughly glean out of such paragraphs of apology or defense of the methodology of dialectical materialism, is that by putting the stress on the materialist side the purer methodology that properly belonged to dialectics in the hands of Hegel (from which Marx avowedly derived his own theory) has been adapted and modified by later Marxists in order to serve or justify an impending revolution.

Now that the high winds of revolution have blown past the country, dialectics is again coming to its own through the help of its present exponents. Although this in itself is acceptable as an encouraging sign of the times, we have still to hope that dialectical methodology itself will receive proper attention so that it could be formulated with less vagueness.

To our way of thinking, the thesis and the antithesis in a given situation have to be equated and treated unitively before the synthesis can be treated naturally. To put emphasis on any one of them would be like wanting to touch the pan of a weighing machine when the true weight is being determined. In other words, materialism should not be accentuated more than what could be perfectly justified by the actual historical necessity of the given moment. When the counterparts are made to neutralize one another without interfering considerations, dialectical

3. Proceedings, p. 118.

methodology may be expected to yield results that could be called correct according to a completely formulated Science of the Absolute which, unfortunately, is still to be openly formulated.

Prof. A. Shishkin, concluding his paper at the same conference, struck rather a pessimistic note when he said:

> It would be Utopia to think that in our day there is possible a general philosophy for all, that the variety and the contradictory character of the philosophical convictions and views could be smelted into an entity acceptable to all people, to all classes and nations.[4]

If dialectical materialism has done great service in bringing the warring elements within the U.S.S.R. under the aegis of a dominant philosophy, it would not be too wrong to hope that, with the correct formulation of dialectical methodology as a complete science with an epistemology and the theory of values proper to it, it might one day help to spell human solidarity and peace. No doctor has any right to say that the patient will die before he is actually dead.

Vyāsa and Marx as Dialecticians

Prof. M. Bakhitov at the same conference made a heartening reference to the teachings of the Bhagavad Gita "as an outstanding example of a philosophical poem" containing "ethical teachings sometimes in a religious form." He made eulogistic reference to the "philosophy and social thought of the great Indian people."[5] Dialectics with materialistic, social and historical bias is only a very limited and partial aspect of the scope of Dialectics taken as a whole, even when free from one-sided weightage.

The glaring ignorance of the nature of the teachings of the Bhagavad Gita revealed in such statements by those who in other

---

4. Proceedings, p. 190.

5. Ibid., p. 154.

respects are sympathetic to Indian thought, has to be laid equally on the shoulders of both Indians who have not commented on the Bhagavad Gita so far in the light of dialectics of which it is perhaps one of the world's greatest masterpieces, and outsiders who still take only a passing interest in such writings.

The eighteen chapters of this great work show how the dialectical method can be applied to different life values covering the whole range of worthwhile human interests, with all the realism of an impending war. The "Yoga" of the Bhagavad Gita is none other than dialectics and it has been methodologically presented as a science there. The limited application of dialectics with a materialist tilt given to it with the vague idea of historical necessity as a thesis with which the synthesis is to be rightly struck, is a form of speculation not far different from the theology of the Middle Ages which it was itself meant to counter, with only this difference, that while heaven served as the thesis in scholastic philosophy, the earth fulfils the same role here. The use of dialectics without tampering with either scale of the balance, according to a scientifically established methodology, is still to come. A telescope can magnify or reduce the apparent size of the moon depending on which end is used. The science of dialectical method must not distort reality one way or the other.

In ushering such a science into being we have much to learn from such textbooks as the Bhagavad Gita.

The Keyword in Dialectical Methodology

Sāmya (sameness) is the keyword put into the mouth of Arjuna, the hero of the Bhagavad Gita, to characterize the fundamental nature of the teaching there. The word as used in Chapter VI, Verse 33 is purposely meant by Vyāsa to characterize the chief feature and secret of dialectics. Earlier in the work (II. 48), in the definition of Yoga itself, Vyāsa states: "Sameness is yoga" (*samatvam yoga ucyate*). The same keyword is further underlined more explicitly. *Sāmya* and *samādhi* (state of identity) are related by definition to the same root. The target to be attained by a Science of the Absolute is supreme identity with the Absolute.

The true balance between thesis and antithesis for the emergent value of the synthesis is what may be said to be implicit in this "sameness" of the Bhagavad Gita context.

Loka-saṁgraha (welfare of society) is the only allusion to the social aspect of life in the whole range of the Bhagavad Gita (III.20, 25) which incidentally and secondarily refers to social thought, as coming anywhere near to Marxist thought. When (in XVIII.66) Arjuna is advised to transcend all social duty and take refuge in the Absolute alone, the supra-social character of the thought in the Bhagavad Gita becomes all the more patent. Notions like justice however come within the natural scope of the Bhagavad Gita as stressed in the concluding verse.

Dialectics in the Bhagavad Gita is a comprehensive method of understanding the Absolute which is unitive and knows no distinction even between the dual aspects of the relative and the absolute treated dualistically. The social question is one of the many questions in life, the whole range of which is brought under the light of dialectical methodology in the Bhagavad Gita.

Sāmya just means agreement, equality, sameness or reducing a conflict in terms of a unity. It corresponds to the synthesis of the Hegel-Marx context. When once understood apart from its particular application, then, as with pure mathematics, the key of dialectical method based on the true synthesis, equation or the cancelling out of counterparts, will open many doors.

Contemporary Marxism as reflected in such statements as quoted above, such as "The criterion of practice is both absolute and relative," is hard to fit backward into the total context of dialectical idealism where it properly belongs. If we should scrutinize the method implicit here it is easy to see that the central concept of *a criterion of practice* is related to two poles of the unitive Absolute, which are referred to as the *relative* and the *absolute* respectively. These may also be referred to as the thesis and antithesis respectively of the notion of the practical criterion which is the unknown principle to be determined as the *synthesis* of the other two. A materialist bias has to be given to this central notion, and revolution has also to be introduced as a progressive factor of evolution, in order to give modernity and scientific finish to the method that is implied. How all these can hang together by one peg is hard to see, except either as a policy suited to a great nation at the present phase of its evolution, or as a speculation stretched beyond limits.

The further elaboration of dialectical methodology would take us outside the scope of methodology proper and involve us in considerations of epistemology and the theory of values which are inseparable for a detailed methodological study. We shall devote separate articles to them under respective headings.

2

The Dialectics of the Gods

A PERFECTED man is the same as a visible God on earth. One and the same person could be the Son of Man and the Son of God at once, as in the case of Jesus. Likewise, all teachers of higher wisdom gain a divine status as that of representatives of God on earth.

A god is superior to the extent that there is the touch of humanity in him, and a mortal can gain by good life an immortal reputation. To be a good rival to God, as Mephistopheles was thought to be, gives even the Devil a respectable status in the context of contemplative spirituality. An insight into the esoterics of the gods would be of help in order to distinguish the plus and minus sides of godhood, and to say what is outside the scope of the contemplative scheme of values, and in order to guide ourselves between the dualities of the sacred and the profane, the godly and the satanic, the permissive and the obligatory, the active and the quiet, ways of contemplative life.

Much mystical doctrine could be derived therefrom. The two ways of traffic between the domain of gods and that of man has been tacitly recognized in all wisdom writings, although such have yet to be properly formulated and made part of a Science of the Absolute. To put Man and God in the correct dialectical perspective proper to both of them at once, is then the first step in understanding the various gods, whether Egyptian, Hellenic, Hindu or Chinese.

Mechanistic Approach Favours Scepticism

The truth of God, seen as it were with overemphasis on the actual, empirical or mechanistic side of life, necessarily leads to a static and closed concept of God which is bound to leave the thinking man of modern times cold and unconvinced about spiritual life altogether.

The logical and ratiocinative reasons advanced for a belief in God sound sterile, one-legged and laboured even in spite of many years of preaching from pulpits or proving through the press. Some of the arguments seem very clever, but are soon forgotten. Passing through the stages of cogitation and meditation, thought becomes frustrated and beats its wings in vain without arriving at the correct contemplative way of dialectics. Mythology and theology, deism and theism are mistrusted nowadays, making of modern man, though dissatisfied, a very respectable type of sceptic.

In disjunct contexts of time or of clime, however, the heritage of human wisdom has always been present. The mysteries, rites, initiations and orgies surviving in different regions to the present day, indicate how even the common man hankers still for some higher or secret knowledge. The human soul, babbling inarticulately, still hopes to formulate all the scattered secrets of this domain into a positive, codified system of thought scientifically stated in universal terms, so that closed idolatries may not demand sacrifices in human blood any more as in the past.

A comparative study of gods, with the myths, songs, rituals and observances connected with them, might help the Absolute Truth make man free, which he is consciously or unconsciously striving for in the name of Happiness, the common goal of all mankind.

Only a properly formulated Science of the Absolute, which will bring together into a systematic whole the scattered secrets found in esoterics the world over, especially in relation to the gods, whether of Olympus in Greece or Mount Kailāsa in the Himalayas, can help the cause of integrated education which humanity stands in need for its security, peace and solidarity. Absolute Truth has to save humanity from the stagnant waters of unbelief prevailing at present, due to closed and static forms of wisdom teaching.

The Two Interpenetrating Worlds of Man and God

Although the domain of Caesar is different from that of God, there is at least one point of contact between them.

The vision of God is not given to man normally, and even Moses was only vouchsafed a passing glimpse of Lord, and that too from behind within a protected position as mentioned in the Bible (Exodus 23.18ff). The Bhagavad Gita (XV.10 and XI.8) refers to the "yogic eye" or the "eye of wisdom" required to see contemplative spiritual secrets. Mythology knows also how disastrous it is for a mere mortal to gaze on the forms of immortals.

Actaeon, the young hunter who happened to look at Artemis bathing in the forest springs, was changed into a stag soon to be torn by his own hounds.

Olympus itself is situated away from human haunts so that mortals may not pry into godly affairs too easily. In spite of all these difficulties Hercules has access to heaven through promotion to godhood, and the god of medicine (Aesculapius) belonged to human and divine worlds at once.

Dionysos is the most versatile and changeful god of the whole Greek pantheon, for he could change at the horizontal level from one form of animal to another, and visit all the vertical levels of the different graded interests that the various other gods were concerned with or responsible for under the leadership of Zeus. He could even pass from death to life at will.

Hermes the Messenger could also travel downwards or upwards at the command of Zeus, the most high god of the twelve

Olympians. Human frailties are found in a magnified form in Eros and Aphrodite.

Bacchus (Dionysos) can touch the lowest and the highest chords in the range of human interests. Hades of the underworld is still a god of Olympus, and the earth goddess Demeter is not too undignified to sit with the bright celestials of heaven, although she might be expected to be of the earth-earthy type to a superlative degree.

Such are some of the secrets of mythology which are available for us to reconstitute and reconstruct the total world of the gods.

Infra-human entities such as the fish and the stag, the snake and the divine bird, the fecund earth and the fertilizing river, as well as mere woman and man, are all included in the contemplative or spiritual hierarchy of presences in the Hindu context. There is even a tortoise and the boar incarnation of Vishnu among the ten forms of God. It is not hard to see that divinities, gods and presences bring together the whole range of human interests into a focal point cosmologically and psychologically at once.

Further, we can see that the normative central notion is the Absolute and that neither mere objectivity nor subjectivity is recognized in the approach to the gods. Instead, we have what may be called the contemplative or dialectical way, in which subject and object come together in terms of value. The various gods of divine entities may thus be looked upon as a vertical series of contemplative interests or values natural and legitimate for man to recognize in the fulfilment of his high purpose in life, viewed both prospectively and retrospectively at once.

We can therefore get started in this study with this simple generalization, namely, that while Caesar's domain consists of a horizontally spread out world of enjoyable things which satisfy man's outer cravings, the world of the gods is a contemplative one where time and pure duration gain primacy over mere objectivity. Olympus, Kailāsa or Vaikuṇṭha are worlds given to pure contemplation in which all ideas, feelings, dispositions and natural instincts have free play. All the strings of the lyre of life could be fingered successively here in harmonious fulfilment, freed from manmade taboos and bans.

Need for Initiation into the Mystery of the Gods

Man's normal world of interests and activities may be said to lie along a horizontal axis where space has primacy, while the worlds in which the gods live may be said to be piled consecutively one above the other.

Natural man, when he is innocent and free like a child, represented by Hermes, may be said to mark the point of contact between the human and the divine worlds. It is because the two worlds are mutually exclusive, except to those who, like children, belong to the kingdom of God, that baptism, conversion, rebirth and initiation become necessary.

All schools of ancient mystery have had their initiates. This only means that the contemplative dialectical way to the higher secrets of wisdom proper are not readily given to man in the normal course of secular education. One has to consciously affiliate oneself to the contemplative way.

After initiation, the status of the gods themselves may be conferred in principle on the initiates so that humans get included in the world of the gods. By conscious affiliation to the contemplative world of values, as seen from the absolutist standpoint, one becomes an equal to God.

The culminating point in the supreme initiation to the mysteries of the gods, is marked in a striking passage in the *Enneads* of Plotinus:

No doubt we should not speak of *seeing*, but instead of *seen* and

> *seer* speak boldly of a simple unity. For in this seeing we neither see nor distinguish nor are there two. The man (the initiate) is changed, no longer himself nor self-belonging; he is merged with the Supreme, sunken into It, one with It; only in separation is there duality. — VI.ix.10

Later in the same *Ennead* he has his famous words:

> This is the life of gods and of godlike and blessed men — liberation from the alien that besets us here, a life taking no pleasure in the things of earth — a flight of the alone to the Alone. — VI.ix.11

Although human life is disposed to move and have its being in the world of horizontal values, by conscious affiliation to the Wisdom of the Absolute, according to a Science of the Absolute, it is possible for man to enter the vertical world of contemplative values and finally achieve identification in spirit with the Absolute who is none other than the Most High God or the Puruṣottama as He is named in the Bhagavad Gita (XV.18).

Enigma or Paradox Normal with the Gods

If God is good, how then comes all the evil of reaction? Theology has not been able to give a square answer to this question, which has been persistently asked through the ages. In reality there is no getting round this enigma or paradox by the ratiocinative method.

Dialectics accommodates paradox and, when the middle ground between opposites is given full scope, dialectical verities emerge into being. The Absolute is both existent and non-existent (*sat* and *asat* in Sanskrit). Zeus is too radiant to be seen and his wrath would be unbearable, but his favour brings the highest good.

In the Indian context, images of gods have many hands, a pair of which might have complementary functions, such as blessing with one and holding aloft a punishing weapon in the other. The mystery of the gods has always the great element of the unexpected. Even the most civilized or proportionately conceived god of the Greek pantheon, Apollo, who in many respects could be contrasted with Dionysos from the point of view of civilized respectability, has the strange appellation of "the Ambiguous," suggesting paradox. Dr. Seltman even goes so far as to generalize and say, "Any study of the origins of the cult of the Olympians reveals the fact that most goddesses and gods show traces of a dual personality."[1]

In none of the gods does the enigmatic or paradoxical element show itself in a more pronounced manner than in Dionysos, whose origins are lost sight of, possibly towards the East. He was the unconventional or heterodox god of mystical abandon and freedom. Both tragedy and comedy are said to have originated round the "temple" or rather the theatre of Dionysos at the foot of the Acropolis at Athens. Though a god, Dionysos had to be saved and brought to life again. His limbs were separated one from the other by the Titans as the myth represents, and, commenting on this myth we read in Plutarch (*de esu carnium*, vii):

> The sufferings and dismemberment told of Dionysos and the audacity of the Titans with regard to him, of the Titans who taste murder, the scoldings the Titans were subjected to and their quick extinction by thunder, all this is part of the pertinent mythology. . . . In effect that part which is not reasonable, indisciplined and violent which is in us as the non-divine but demoniac is what the ancients have called the Titans and it is this part which is subjected to scoldings and punishment.[2]

It has always been an open secret therefore that the world of the gods tried to relate cosmology, psychology and ethics into one whole. As Dr. Seltman again generalizes, "Thoughts about Deity

1. Charles Seltman, *The Twelve Olympians*, Pan Books, 1952, p. 92.
2. Victor Magnien, *Les Mysteries d' Eleusis*, Payot Paris, translated, p. 130.

tend to correspond to human interests and emotions, ambitions and loves."[3] The author concludes his chapter on Zeus with the following pithy sentence:

> It is for humanism that Zeus ultimately stands.[4]

From Dionysos to the Moheṅjo-Dāṛo Śiva

Before they can see the dialectical revaluation of the gods of the Mediterranean region which resulted from the mingling of secret mystical doctrines into the Neo-Platonic philosophy about two thousand years ago, the Hellenist, Egyptologist and Indologist have first to visualize the spice-wine axis that reached from South India through Alexandria and Palestine to Greece and Rome.

The role of the god Dionysos bears a strange resemblance to that of the crescent wearing, skin-dressed, twig and flame-carrying frenzied god of death and life, known as the Tāndava Nataraja or Śiva of South Indian origin. This is not the first time here that such a possible link has been suggested, and, although Indian orthodoxy has resented the association of their holy Siva with the seemingly licentious god of wine, Bacchus, or "Evoe" (as they shout his name in the Dionysiac orgies), the kinship is striking. Seltman explains the difference when he says:

> The Greeks were very fortunate, since mysticism learnt through Dionysos was not comprehended by way of abnegation and mortification of the flesh, but by way of oblivion and abandonment to the body's clean desires.[5]

The atmosphere of the two gods in question becomes more strikingly similar still, when, describing the sacrifices and rituals associated with this ancient god of mysterious origin in the East, the same author continues:

3. *The Twelve Olympians*, p. 53.
4. Ibid., p. 50.
5. Ibid., p. 170.

> The blood of the goat runs out to the altar down to the pavement. Strange that either fasting or eating raw meat, the scourge or the thyrsos (the twig with ivy on top), the toiled bell or the beaten drum, the body buried in the hooded habit or the naked limbs dancing upon the mountain top, may equally produce a sense of mystical union with God.[6]

One has to wander about in the Catacombs, in the islands of Cyprus, Crete, Sicily, or the scattered archipelago off the Greek coast or around the estuary of the Nile, to soak properly into the melting pot of cultures and mysteries that wafted over from different points of the compass, at the time, roughly, when philosophers such as Ammonius Saccus, Plotinus, Philo the Jew, Origen and Clement of Alexandria, Porphyry, Iamblichus the Syrian theologian and others contributed together to a doctrinal body based on the various gods worshipped in those regions in their time. A comparative study of religio-mystical doctrines of South India and the Mediterranean regions would be of fruitful interest to the modern sceptic who wishes to understand globally the whole range of spiritual wisdom on a revised world basis.

Ascending and Descending Dialectics Implied in Myths

Initiation ritual into the mysteries of the gods has made it evident that what is true of the gods is also true of the soul of man in its ascent or descent from bondage or freedom. Hints which are plentiful in the mystical literature of the day are unmistakable in regard to the ascent and descent of the soul of man. The various gods woven into the antique mythological fabric enable the thinker, endowed with even a small degree of imaginative intuition, to see clearly spiritual progress as understood then.

While the outward language of popular myth supplies the warp, the woof consists of subtler contemplative verities which could not be stated as numbered articles of faith without making the letter dead.

6. *The Twelve Olympians*, p. 176.

Dialectics has always to be understood in living terms like an ever-flowing stream of wisdom in its course of ever-creative becoming. Whole epics like Dante's *Divine Comedy* and Milton's *Paradise Lost* have been found necessary to work out the details of the ascent or descent of the soul or of spiritual progress generally. The same dialectical frame of reference is to be discerned in modified forms in works like Goethe's *Faust* where a range of worlds of value systems, piled one over the other in a vertical series, is to be found.

As we cannot go into elaborate details here, we shall quote again a paragraph from Magnien's *Mysteries of Eleusis*:

> The disappearance of Persephone, taken by Hades, and carried away to Inferno, represents the descent of the soul into the world of generation; Dionysos torn into pieces by the Titans is the soul which becomes multiple by becoming present in different parts of the body; Prometheus attached to a rock and the Titans who devour Dionysos, who is consumed with avidity in Tartary, that means the soul attached to the body which is itself attached to the earth; Hercules engaged in many tasks, that is the soul which prepares itself for its deliverance; Apollo the god who purifies and Athena the goddess who saves, permit the soul to gather once again its strength; Demeter brings back the soul to its first source.[7]

Read together with the mystical doctrine that initiation is a form of death and that the final initiation as we have noted consists of the "flight of the alone to the Alone," we can get the skeleton framework and the mode of operation of the ascent or descent of the soul in its spiritual progression within the world of the Olympic gods. And in passing, we note that there is no fundamental difference between the idea here and the wisdom doctrines of the Vedic context extending into Vedanta in a revalued form as known in India itself.

---

7. *Les Mysteries d' Eleusis*, p. 68.

Vedantic Absolutism Independent of Deism as well as Theism

Vedantic Absolutism is the result of the revaluation of the relativistic approach of the Vedas. The cosmological and psychological frame of reference is, however, common to both. Belief in any god, holiness, piety and duty are all foreign to the Upanishadic way of life which belongs to Vedanta proper. Pantheism, polytheism and henotheism can all be accommodated with the open and universally valid dynamism of the Vedanta, and it is quite in order even to dispense with an Īśvara or demiurge if the philosophical attitude in the seeker of wisdom is sound and proper.

Īśvara (God) is referred to only in the third person in the Bhagavad Gita (XVIII.16) while Chapter XII, verses 5 and 20 read together will show that deism or theism are only second best alternatives to a true Vedantin. Even Jaimini, the basic authority on the anterior critique (Pūrva Mīmāṁsā), accepts the frame of Vedic relativism in the absolutist context and maintains neutral indifference to theism or atheism. This is pointed out by K.F. Leidecker in this short note on Mīmāṁsā in Rune's *Dictionary of Philosophy* (Bombay, 1957). "It . . . is indifferent to a concept of God." The Sāṁkhya system is a rational branch which is free from theism (called the *Nirīśvara Sāṁkhya*), and when we know that Vedanta is even one flight of steps higher in the scale of the development of dialectical wisdom as formulated by Bādarāyaṇa (reputed author of the *Brahma-Sūtras*), it is not hard to see that gods are only permissible requisites for Vedāntic discipline, and not at all obligatory.

However, this does not mean that the methodological and epistemological frame of reference common to both Veda and Vedanta, as also to the four other systems, is to be discarded. Just as the dialectics of the Old Testament continues valid in revalued terms in the New Testament of Christianity, so also in the teaching of Advaita Vedanta. Vedanta aims at expressing the Absolute unitively as a final triumph of Absolutism over relativism by the process of double negation.

The whole of the Bhagavad Gita may be considered as a text in which the various aspects of such a revaluation are developed stage by stage through its eighteen masterly chapters.

Those who wish to examine in detail the nature of the revaluation in all its intermediary implications would do well to study the *Bṛhadāraṇyaka Upanishad* where gods, rituals and secret doctrines interlace interestingly as the process of revaluation of Vedic Deism took forward strides. Not without a certain touch of sarcasm does this Upanishad allude (I.iv.10) to the uneasiness of the gods if men should get out of their possessive control through wisdom in respect of That (the Absolute).

The Vedāntically Revalued Gods of the Indian Context

By the writings of the chief teachers on Vedanta, the status of the Most High God or the Puruṣottama with full Absolute stature, has been conferred on three divinities of antiquity on the Indian soil, without a review of which our consideration of the dialectics of the gods would be incomplete.

The Śiva family, which historically is perhaps the most ancient of the three, with Śiva and the dialectical implications of his two sons Gaṇeśa and Subrahmaṇya, and the more unitive aspect of Śiva as the Ardha-Nārīśvara, have already been touched upon in another study.[8]

Here we shall only add that, like Dionysos, this God fills the whole range or field in which the notion of the Absolute may be said to live and move. The lowest rungs of the ladder of human interests, the most wonderful powers of a Supreme God, and

8. See the articles, "The Androgynous God of South India" and "The Philosophy of the Divine Family of Śiva" in *Wisdom* by the present author: D.K. Printworld, New Delhi, 1994.

exploits that belong to the everyday level of human beings are all attributed to Śiva, while he remains with his middle eye in eternal contemplation. He is the unconventional God of mystic abandon and fulfilment. He may be said to fill the heavenly and the nether regions at once by his dynamic presence. Instead of being subject to time, he wears time itself as snakes round his neck while he dances with the crescent moon in his matted locks. Those who understand Dionysiac frenzy in the West can easily imagine what this God of Absolutist status represents. Like Olympus for Zeus, Śiva's domain is in high Kailāsa in the Himalayas.

We can make only a passing reference to Vishnu, who lives in Vaikuṇṭha on the eastern peak of Mount Meru. The snake here with a thousand hoods is called Ananta (the Endless) who represents pure duration, on which Vishnu, ever in meditative repose, reclines. The snake itself is represented as floating in an ocean of milk, which stands for the pure life-value of abundance or mercy which is boundless. Vishnu is the continuation of the pre-Vedic Pañcarātra tradition which had Ādi-Nārāyaṇa and Vāsudeva in its anterior and posterior developments. Like Apollo or Phoebus, Vishnu is a civilized or refined god with no excesses like Śiva, and he has consorts who resemble Athena more than any other Olympian goddess.

Brahmā is more of a cosmological deity and is given a relativistic position only, as seated in a lotus arising form the navel of the reclining Vishnu we have pictured above. Brahmā as a god has four (sometimes five) faces looking at the four directions (and above). As a member of this trio of divinities (*Trimūrti*) his status would be fully absolute only if we should treat the god as representing the Vedas or as the Golden Germ of Creation (*Hiraṇya-garbha*), which is still only the lower aspect of the Absolute, with its own higher dialectical counterpart, *Para-Brahman*, which is not a deity, but being in the neuter gender, stands for the neutral Vedantic Absolute.

The term *śabda* (verbal) *Brahma* is said to refer to the Vedas, but the philosopher who seeks the Absolute is said to transcend this Brahmā of the Vedas by his sheer interest in pure Absolutist wisdom, as stated in the Bhagavad Gita (VI.44), the relevant part of which verse reads:

> By merely being one desirous of yoga (dialectical wisdom) one transcends (the domain of) the articulated (Vedic) aspect of Brahmā (as a god).

Para and *Apara Brahman* which refer to the transcendent and immanent aspects of the Absolute, or rather the absolutist and the relativistic aspects of the Absolute, have to be dialectically revalued again in terms of the neutral Absolute.

Although the three gods Brahmā, Vishnu and Śiva have equality of status as members of the triune divinities fused into one called the Trimūrti, who is a composite Godhead popularly adored by the masses of India, *nirguṇa* (pure) *Brahman* or *Brahman* which is both immanent and transcendent at once (described as the *para-apara*) is alone to be given the full Absolute status side by side with the other two members of the trio, who within the Trimūrti enjoy a fully revalued status as representing the Absolute.

If to these three we should add a goddess such as Sarasvatī who represents Sophia or wisdom, and give a place to the central Sun (Pūṣan or Sūrya) as the adorable representative of the Absolute, we shall have summarily touched upon all the principal Upanishadic divinities.

The divine or semi-divine entities of the three worlds of the Hindu psycho-cosmology are legion. The followers of the Guru Madhvācārya give graded positions to all Hindu gods in their hierarchy, always presided over by Vishnu as Zeus rules over all the different divinities in Olympus. We shall only just mention the instance of the *tulasī* (the sacred basil) plant which enjoys the status of the consort of Vishnu and is worshipped as a presence by the followers of Madhva.

Avatāra and Vyūha Doctrines

The dialectical way of wisdom, as it pertains to divinities and divine presences, has the theory of the *avatāra* (descent of God on earth) for the salvation of mankind. The *Rāmāyaṇa* and the *Mahābhārata* are built on such a theory, but such Purāṇas (traditional lore), though containing Vedāntic teaching, are not taken very seriously by those who claim to be more advanced in their ideas of spiritual life.

The Bhāgavata Religion, built around the God Vāsudeva, flourished in India three or four centuries before Christ. According to this religion, besides the highest God Vāsudeva, there were three others in descending order, which were considered hypostatic representatives of the highest God, and were named Saṁkarṣaṇa, Pradyumna and Aniruddha. The doctrine of *vyūha* presupposes that one and the same God could manifest himself in different hypostatic levels.

Finally, if we add to the idea of the *avatāra* and the *vyūha* doctrines just mentioned, the possibility of the manifestation of the Absolute in various presences on the Earth, such as those enumerated serially in the tenth chapter of the Bhagavad Gita (verse 20 onwards), we shall have touched upon almost all the aspects of contemplative divine beings in the world of Indian antiquity.

The Vedanta of Rāmānuja and Image Worship

The extreme limit of the possibility of the dialectical approach to divinities and divine presences can be found in the writings of the Guru Rāmānujācārya of South India (*c.* eleventh century).

If we concede, as we have already mentioned, that the Absolute is a supreme paradox where contraries and contradictions naturally get effaced, it should be possible and more than permissible, to see God in any consecrated object on earth. God is omnipresent and can be invoked anywhere by a devotee who knows the right way to reach Him.

Ramanuja's position here, which may be said sometimes to excel Saṅkara's in the matter of a thoroughgoing application of the dialectical method to the problem of the Absolute, is summed up in the following paragraph by Professor O. Lacombe of the University of Paris, with which we shall for the present conclude our review of the gods or divinities familiar to us and as regarded in the light of the dialectics of Absolutist Wisdom:

> Narayana consents to (an even) greater humility (than that of descent to save mankind); he wishes to inhabit the stone, the lump of bronze or wood of the images that we might set up for sustaining the first babblings of our prayer. By that is justified the adoration of consecrated idols; by means of a body consisting of glory, Īśvara (God) resides there specially, in order from there to receive our homage and to manifest to us sensibly his presence. Although omniscient, he appears as if ignorant; although spiritual, as if material; although master of himself, as if he were within the power of men; although all-powerful; as if powerless, although entirely free from all wants, as if feeling wants; although master, as if servant; although invisible, as if visible; although beyond reach, as if within reach.[9]

Dialectics cannot be pushed any further in bringing the Absolute nearer to human life by common consent of both the sides, as suggested in the Bhagavad Gita (III.11):

> With this nourish ye the gods, and let the gods nourish ye; Thus nourishing one the other, ye shall attain to supreme Good.

9. O. Lacombe, *L' Absolu selon le Vedanta*, Paris, 1937, translated, p. 328.

3

The Dialectics of Romance and Tragedy

ART begins when the Absolute is imitated in creative action. Action can refer to the inner world as well as to the outer. It can have a field or ground both cosmological and psychological. The Self is its living core. When we sit back and enjoy a play that is filled with action, we are sometimes moved to tears or overpowered by laughter. Our own interior is what the play represents as possibilities in a fluid form. There is an interplay that takes place subtly between overt or innate action whether subjectively or objectively or both, in the harmonious unravelling of which the greatness of the artist consists. An element of conflict or complicating factor, whether in the mild form of a frustrated love or in the intense form of a life and death struggle, is common to both tragedy and comedy. Romance and tragedy both arise from the same stem of the tree of life.

In the West the mystery rites, round the figure of Dionysos, offered the archetypal pattern for the later development of both tragedy and romance or comedy, as also of that intermediate type under which much modern literature could be included indifferently. The split between classicism and romanticism after the eighteenth century, of which latter school Victor Hugo may be said to be the champion or high priest, was merely in the name of greater "liberalism in art" as he himself explains in his preface to *Hernani* (para 2) which play itself holds much in common with Greek tragedy.

In Oriental literary tradition pure tragedy with its gruesome outwardness tended to be toned down. Tragic elements became blended and subdued more harmoniously in a general mystical and contemplative setting. In Kālidāsa's *Kumārasambhavam,* where the central figure is Śiva instead of Dionysos, tragic and romantic elements are brought into focal unity with great artistic perfection. Human life mixes freely with the supra- or infra-human, representing life as a confection of both ingredients.

It is dialectics which enters into the creative technique of art in general and of tragedy and romance in particular. The world of art is, in the first place, a world apart. It has much to do with mental distraction, reverie or contemplation in which dialectical laws prevail. Conflict or agony (agon) as between the Self and the non-Self or other dichotomous aspects of the reality which is no other than the Absolute, is at the core of tragedy which gave birth to comedy and romance in turn. The principle of Dithyrambos associated with the dancing god Dionysos also known as "The One of Two Doors" is another secret known to the Greeks whose significance is to be sought through dialectics.

Similarly, the principle of *nemesis* in which divinities like Zeus and Hades take sides, has to be understood in the light of dialectics. How Chance, Providence or Fate enter into tragedy or romance without violating laws of poetic justice is again a subject for intuition of the contemplative order to explain or resolve. The excesses of revenge or retribution on the one hand, and of the Bacchanalian orgiac elements on the other hand, which are to be found in all classical or romantic drama have to be fitted into a coherent scheme of infra-human, human, or supra-human life.

Whether in Kālidāsa, Shakespeare, Milton, Dante, Goethe or Hugo, a subtle dialectics is implied in their bold creations. To miss this essence would be to ignore the best flavour of art altogether and with it what is the most precious part of the wisdom heritage of humanity. The highest role of art, especially in romance or tragedy, is not to "assert eternal Providence, and justify the ways of God to men," as Milton put it.[1]

Such are some of the random items which indicate broadly the scope and purpose of the present essay.

Subject and Object of the Principle of Mimesis

Both Plato and his great disciple Aristotle conceived of art generally as a form of imitation. With Plato it was a perfect World of the Intelligibles which was the original imitated. Aristotle thought that imitation referred to reality here and now as implied in existence itself without rising to the world of ideas. These two positions have first to be reconciled dialectically. Both the statements are true when understood in the spirit of dialectics. Whether we say, "a mother's son" or, conversely, "the son's mother" we refer to one and the same central relationship. The central verity implied in both the propositions is the same, as when cause and effect, master and servant, and similar dialectical pairs are unitively understood.

Mimesis is a double-doored, double-faced or double-edged principle which works both ways. The secret of the Dithyrambos to which we shall come presently, pertains to the same dialectical order. When we read in *Hamlet*, "The play's the thing wherein I'll catch the conscience of the King"[2] we will notice that an equal status is given to the objective and the subjective aspects. Art holds up a mirror to life and life can be a mirror to art likewise. The play here and the conscience revealed in the features of the King are to be looked upon as dialectical counterparts which are brought together and equated so as to reveal the Absolute Reality which is neither subjective nor objective.

---

1. *Paradise Lost*, line 25.
2. Act II, ii 633.

Secret of Dithyramb in Tragedy and Romance

Aristotle wrote: "Tragedy as also comedy was at first mere improvization — the one (tragedy) originated with the leaders of the Dithyramb."[3] Dithyrambos was one of the names of Dionysos who is the Leaper, the Dancer and the Life-Giver. Dithyramb is the song of the birth of Dionysos sung at the spring festival.

That the suggestion of this name referred to a double-birth of a twice-born spirit of spring-time was well known to the Greeks. But speculation on the etymology of this word is still in progress even in modern times, as is evidenced by the following extract from *Ancient Art and Ritual* by Dr. Jane Allen Harrison. She writes:

> By a false analogy they explained the word Dithyrambos as meaning, 'He of the double door.' They were quite mistaken; Dithyrambos, modern philology tells us, is the Divine Leaper, Dancer and Life-Giver.[4]

To those who are familiar with the dialectical notion of the eternal present which is ever being born while ever dying, the double-door device attributed to the God Dionysos as the spirit of Spring or pure Becoming, will not be an enigma as it seems to be to this author. She seems to recognize tacitly the value of the original Greek etymology, however, when she continues in the same paragraph as follows:

> But their false etymology is important to us, because it shows that they believed the Dithyrambos was the twice-born. Dionysos was born, they fabled once, of his mother, like all men; one of his father's thigh like no man.

This mythological explanation, in reality, is only a vulgarized version of the dialectical verity of pure duration which is known

---

3. *Poetics.*
4. p. 104.

even in modern times to philosophers like Bergson, besides being known once in pre-Socratic times to Parmenides and Zeno.

In fact, the mystery of Dionysos refers to the absolute nature of the essence or substance of Reality which is both a Wonder and a high Value. Those who are familiar with the Tāṇḍava (Leaper) or the Naṭarāja (Dancer) who is Śiva, the Eastern counterpart of the same Dionysos, will have no difficulty in seeing the dialectical verity which this myth represents. Modern philosophically minded persons who can understand a statement such as "a Monad has no windows," must have no real difficulty with the two doors of becoming, one opening prospectively and the other opening retrospectively into the domain of eternal pure duration. As in the problems of the one and the many, a subtle dialectics enters herein which refers to a way of wisdom outmoded and gone into disuse. The double-phased secret of the Dithyramb as applied to tragedy and to romances like *Hernani*, which are made almost of the same tragic stuff, thus becomes solved in the light of dialectics.

Unitive Treatment of Action and Actor

If the secret of romance and tragedy is to be extracted and full benefits derived from the lesson, we have to learn to view the actor and the action of the play or romance as brought under one unitive dialectical treatment. The action is not to be understood as separate from the actor, or even from the setting in which the actor is put. They can effectively set off one another or belong to subject and object at once. An immobile actor as the hero in *Prometheus Bound* as represented by Aeschylus, fulfils requirements of both actor and action as they are to be understood unitively and together in the sense we mean here.

Prof. W.J. Oates, Professor of Classics at Princeton University, utterly misses the significance of this immobility of Prometheus when he writes:

> In the *Prometheus Bound* Aeschylus was faced with a difficult problem of dramaturgy since he had to build a play in which his central character could not move in the very literal sense of the word. Consequently the poet found himself considerably limited in scope and was forced practically to eliminate from his play anything which we might call "action." Aeschylus solves the problem by introducing several characters who in one way or another set off the central figure.[5]

If we remember that tragedy rose out of the Mysteries of Eleusis where the action was the death of Dionysos and his rising therefrom, it is not hard to see how Prometheus, as the central figure here, conforms to the same archetypal pattern or type of action which is of the essence of tragedy itself.

Mobility and immobility are meant to be dialectically juxtaposed in this central figure of Prometheus, who will be unbound in a later drama belonging to the same series as intended by the author. The implied action of stealing the fire of heaven for the benefit of mankind of a benignant and suffering servant of mankind in agony, contains intense virtual or innate action which this modern critic fails to appreciate or misses.

The hero and his action here have to be understood against the drama's own background of myth and allegory which conforms to an interplay of value factors which must be understood in the light of both ascending and descending dialectics. The wrath of Zeus on high and the degradation in which mankind lived without fire, are the dialectical value counterparts within whose range the agony of Prometheus is depicted masterfully. No overt action, however ingeniously conceived, could ever be an effective substitute to this movement of the spirit in its intensity of tragic suffering, which is a form of action in inaction. The apology of the critic for Aeschylus can thus be seen to be quite out of place. Similarly it might be asked what action there is in the tears shed

5. *Seven Famous Greek Plays*, tr. p. 4.

by a banished Sītā of Bhavabhūti or in the inner anguish of a Śakuntalā in the central scene of Kālidāsa's play. Tragedy could consist equally in an inner or outer event when art is conceived according to correct dialectical requirements as it always is in the best instances. The actor's inner anguish could be offset by outer events and vice versa, bringing action and actor into unitive interplay.

Drama and Drumenon as Interchangeable Terms

The distinction between pure and practical action is a dialectical subtlety which we have to grasp with clarity in regard to drama understood as consisting of overt action with a practical end and drama meant as an end in itself. The Greek terms Drama, denoting something done, and Drumenon, also meaning something done, but in the context of ritual, were both of the same origin.

The Greeks acted their tragedies round an altar as an offering to Dionysos who himself or his high priest was required to be present on such annual solemn festivals. It was almost obligatory for a respectable Athenian to attend this ritual. This circumstance throws light on the same problem of overt and innate action just mentioned. An Alcestis on the stage who is brought back from the hands of Death hardly does any overt act herself, but her innate action in a virtual or potential form is the centre of all active interest. Thus there are two actions: one that could be said to be what is natural to a Herakles or an Atlas or other titans, and the other that consists of silent tears, maybe of a suffering hero or heroine. Prometheus himself represented the middle of the scale in which action could move only vertically as he was rock-fixed between hypostatic and hierophantic value worlds. His opposition to Zeus is evident when he calls him "the new tyrant of heaven"[6] and his interest in the world here below of mortals is expressed through the chorus device in the lines addressed to him:

6. *Seven Famous Greek Plays*, p. 13.

Ay, fearing not Zeus, in self-will
Too much thou honorest mortals.[7]

Thus in a vertical scale of action reaching from the world of the Olympian gods to that of mere mortals, is the amplitude within which the agony of Prometheus moves. His action is neither all overt nor merely virtual, but real in a unitive or centrally neutral sense. Bacchus himself, in the later and more mature work of Euripides, as represented by Dionysos, has no action as such. His excellence merely consists in eluding all effects of action brought against him by the power of Pentheus who represents in himself horizontal aspects of action. The vertical and horizontal aspects of dramatic action are very cleverly contrasted in *The Bacchae* of Euripides. The intended contrast may be seen from the examination of a few lines from the drama, when Dionysos finds fault with Pentheus in the following words:

Come, perverse man, greedy for sights you
should not see,
impatient for deeds you should not do.[8]

As against this horizontal aspect of life or action hinted at here we have Dionysos describing his own attitude to life when he says on coming out of the dark dungeon into which Pentheus threw him:

I alone with effortless ease delivered myself.[9]

The Axes of Reference

In the structure of romance and tragedy a tragic hero or two romantic heroes, one a man and other a woman, are to be placed at the very core of the composition. They may be exposed to

---

7. *Seven Famous Greek Plays*, p. 23.
8. Euripides, *Bacchae and Other Plays*, Penguin, 1954, p. 213.
9. Ibid., p. 200.

conflicts as between outer and inner or higher and lower worlds. Horizontal action may develop round them, or the action may lie in the purer domain of feelings or passions which trace their course feebly or strongly in time or duration.

All dramatic structure can be examined with these axes of reference in the mind of the keen critic who would then discover the unitive and subtle dialectical pattern which underlies all the great masterpieces of creation of this kind whether called romantic, lyric, or tragic. *A Midsummer Night's Dream, Hernani* or *Hamlet* may be examined in the light of these axes of reference. That Greek drama was conceived with the same frame of reference would be patent to the keen critic any time. Vertical worlds of value systems are piled one on the other in works like Goethe's *Faust,* which imitates Dante's *Divine Comedy,* from which Milton in his *Paradise Lost* might have also gained inspiration.

Serial worlds, mundane or celestial, vertically arranged, with interests of the here and now giving the centre of each such system its proper embellishment in the form of flesh and blood (which latter is the horizontal aspect as should belong to the vertical value at each given level), such is the structure of the great creations of masterminds who in their bold flights of imagination seek to assert Providence and justify the ways of God to man.

The discussion of examples would take us beyond the legitimate limits of this essay. Only slight indications can be attempted here.

Let us take *A Midsummer Night's Dream,* so popular with the scholastic world. Oberon and Puck are space-minded spirits. They live in a spring or maypole world of colourful luxury of which Bottom brings up the extremely earthy tail end. When Oberon sings:

> We the globe can compass soon
> Swifter than the wandering moon

or when Puck says:

"I'll put a girdle round about the earth in forty minutes", there is no mistaking the touch of Bacchus and that of the spring festival they represent. In other words, they belong to a horizontal axis of life values, as apart from more enduring values which have to be related to the vertical axis or pure scale of values within the core of the life of man.

When the horizontal has been thus distinguished, it would be easier to see what values belong to the more mystical or contemplative world which the youthful yet tragic god Dionysos represents in his own person. When re-read in the light of the above remarks, *The Bacchae* of Euripides would yield much evidence that there are two distinct yet interpenetrating value systems which co-exist in harmony in all great dramatic creations.

The Three Unities Applied to the Core of Drama

Like the Self, the core of drama is to be determined and correctly fixed by means of three unities, namely, those of time, place and action. The ritualistic and idolatrous origin of drama which we have referred to already must be responsible for the insistence of the three unities so rigidly in classical times. At the time of the romantic revolt this was somewhat relaxed and modified but not altogether abandoned. Greater latitude or liberality was allowed to the free-lance knights-errant in the domain of art. It was also the case with reformed religion in Europe.

In the rules of the Tantra of India we have the same insistence on time, place and ritualistic action to be focused together to one point of an existence or spiritual presence. The Absolute was thus given a local habitation and a name, although it was an airy nothing. Drama was to be the meeting point of the theoretical Absolute as well as the practical one. Like ritual when correctly applied to the Absolute, art was an end in itself. Its value was both mediate and immediate. Art was a bridge on which the human soul could pass backwards or forwards between the relative and absolute poles of the Mystery of the Unknown. When not contaminated by mere mercantilism or commercialism, all pure drama must still adhere to this high purpose of interpreting the ways of God to Man.

Even when there happen to be two heroes, or a hero and a heroine as in works that were not tragically conceived in the classical sense, but in a more liberalized version of the same, the interest has to be centralized in both of them enclosed in brackets, unitively as it were, if drama is to fulfil this high role as it did in the hands of the great classical masters. Hugo's hero Hernani has Doña Sol the heroine as his dialectical counterpart, and the interest is round these two personalities taken together. They are to be looked upon as the obverse and reverse of the same soul. When the midnight hour strikes in the last scene of the last act we find Don Ruy Gomez rising to truly tragic height representing the Fate or Providence which really stands for the Absolute in the lives of men. The requirements of a tragedy which Aristotle referred to in his definition, could be seen to apply equally to this part of Hugo's great creation as to the case of the best examples of Greek tragedy proper. The definition reads as follows:

> Tragedy is an imitation of an action of high importance, complete and of a certain amplitude; in language enhanced by distinct and varying beauties; acted, not narrated; by means of pity and fear effecting its purgation of these emotions.

In the case of *Hernani* the fear of the inexorable hand of Fate and the pity of two loving souls who drink poison from the hands of each other, to drop dead side by side at the very striking of their nuptial hour, effects the same purgation that touches the high watermark of romance and tragedy at once.

Essential Counterparts of a Tragic Situation

Tragedy which is of the essence of drama revolves round a hero of tragic stature. It depends on a subtle dialectical situation into which counterparts of Absolute Reality of the philosophical or contemplative order enter or interact.

It requires the prophet, philosopher or poet to discover the crux or essence of the situation involved in true tragedy. The madman and the lover can also be admitted into this company of raving, loud-voiced, exalted, excited or frenzied personalities who resemble mystics or philosophers and belong to the world of tragedy as characters therein.

The tragic hero is the Śiva or the Dionysos principle which represents human life as understood *in toto*. The counterparts of such an absolutist character have a polarity, dichotomy or ambivalence as between the two reciprocal aspects of the Absolute itself, one of which could be labelled negative and the other positive.

These counterparts present varying degrees of unity or conflict. Vertically viewed they merge into one another without overtly tragic circumstances developing round them. When viewed horizontally or slanting in any other intermediate angle, tragic situations develop according to the degree of deviation from the vertical axis.

The tragic situation between an Othello and a Desdemona involves the murder of the latter through a jealousy which attains to an absolute status and takes possession of the whole person of the hero in the play. *Alcestis* presents quite another picture. Instead of a wife suspected of infidelity there is here a wife willing to die to save the life of a husband. She is brought back to life by the intervention of a Herakles who is both a titan and a god at once. He represents Dionysos in a milder form. When two lovers commit double suicide because a third factor called Fate intervenes to separate them cruelly in this life, to promise unity in the life hereafter, as in the case of Hugo's *Hernani*, to which we have already alluded, the split or tragic situation consists of the horizontal aspects of life values only. The bridal bed on which they did not lie implies only a here and now value which was frustrated in this tragic romance of dual negation. In *Alcestis,* however, double assertion is the secret. Her spirit was tuned and dedicated to a higher value grounded in the pure or vertical Absolute. The horizontal expression here is almost nil as dramatic action in Shakespearean sense. Her touching adieu to her own children and her ceremonial preparation of herself are the only expressions depicted. Even these may still be said to lie in the ritualistic, symbolic, perceptual or purely vertical axis of dramatic movement. In *The Bacchae* of Euripides the vertical movement is perfectly represented in the role of Dionysos, who may be said to act and not to act at one and the same time throughout the play.

Tragedy as Dramatization of the Mysteries of Eleusis

The Mysteries of Eleusis touched the culminating point indicated by the saying of Plotinus concerning "the flight of the alone to the Alone." It is as if the dewdrop slipped into the shining sea, to put the same secret in its more Eastern context. The phoenix which gets burnt to rise again alive from the same fire indicates the same secret as enshrined in the myth or allegory of the Near East. A careful critical scrutiny of the structure of the scheme of values involved in great dramatic compositions and the role played by the various characters, and more especially the Greek choruses which are brought into the play for supplying the philosophy of the author himself as the play unravels, to make the drama significant and meaningful in the wisdom context, would reveal beyond doubt that the drama in its best instances shares and teaches the high hope of eternal life that distinguishes mankind.

No drama could afford to miss this aspect. A drama would be inferior to the extent that it glosses over this timeless and climeless reality. Even in a drama like Hugo's *Hernani,* the double tragedy of the death of the two lovers is not without this idea of resurrection, at least suggested before they die. Doña Sol, still pale and dying while her lover, who is also in the throes of death, watches on in pity and sympathy, says the following hopeful words:

> *Vers des clartés nouvelles*
> *Nous allons tout a l'heure ensemble ouvrir nos ailes;*
> *Partons d'un vol egal vers un monde meilleur.*
>
> Toward new clarities
> We shall be going soon together to open our wings;
> Let us depart in equal flight towards a better world.
>
> — Act V

The transfiguration, passion or ascension of Christ, strangely conforms to the dialectics understood and implicit in the best examples of Greek tragedy. In fact, this was the most precious part of the wisdom of the ancients, which left its imprint equally on Pagan or Christian, Jewish or Gentile, literature of the Mediterranean civilization. When compared with the absolutist doctrines and artistic creations built round the figure of Śiva, the counterpart of Dionysos, who may be said to belong to South India, the student is bound to see striking resemblances which establish a common bond between the innermost wisdom teachings of both these cultural growths.

The nature of the common dialectical secret involved could best be brought out here, without getting lost ourselves in subtle theorizations, by merely quoting the following words put into the mouth of a prophet, as he is referred to in *The Bacchae*, whose author Euripides lived about 480-406 BCE. Teiresias the prophet addresses the following to his maternal grandson Pentheus, who objected to Dionysos and the doings of the Bacchae. The wise man justifies the Bacchae in the following words:

> There are two powers, young man, which are supreme in human affairs: first, the Goddess Demeter; she is the Earth — call her by what name you will; and she supplies mankind with solid food. Second, Dionysos the son of Semele; the blessing he provides is

> the counterpart to the blessing of bread; he discovered and bestowed on men the service of drink, the juice that streams from the vine-cluster; men have but to take their fill of wine, and the sufferings of an unhappy race are banished, each day's troubles are forgotten in sleep — indeed this is our only cure for the weariness of life. *Dionysos, himself a god, is poured out in offering to the gods, so that through him mankind receives blessing.*[10]

If we take care here that the wine and the offering of it is to be understood as a symbolic rite rather than as a real act in its modern sense, it would not be difficult to see how this resembles the rite of the Eucharist of Christianity which was formulated in the same region several centuries later. The grace of God in material form is not unknown in the context of the Tāntric ritual in India, either. The last sentence (italicized) which refers to the god himself as an offering to the gods, is fully dialectical in its import, to leave which unnoticed would be to miss the whole point of this essay.

* * *

From the days of Aristotle down, literary criticism has made bold efforts to define and fix the characteristics of Romance and Tragedy. Much speculative subtlety has been allowed and tolerated. The nature of the tragic hero, what makes for the tragic situation, the action that has tragic grandeur or stature, not to speak of what is often referred to as the true spirit or experience of Tragedy, have all been profusely dwelt upon by various critics and writers both ancient and modern.

Having come to the point of recognizing that there is a deep, unitive mystery underlying both Romance and Tragedy as understood from the most ancient times, we shall here try to take a closer view in order to bring to light the inner structure and the dialectical interplay of the ambivalent factors involved, and thus

---

10. Euripides, *Bacchae and Other Plays*, p. 120.

see the plan of drama in better relation with human life. The Absolute understood in all its bearings, whether cosmological or psychological, has to be given a central place in aesthetics if the subject is to be treated as having universally valid norms in a world context free from cultural parochialisms and prejudices.

Wisdom Inspired both Philosophy and Art

Art and philosophy had their common source in Wisdom. *Kavi* (poet) in Sanskrit is synonymous with *jñānī* (wisdom-seer) and in the Greco-Roman context Socrates and Euripides had much common life together. It is said of Socrates that "he seldom went to the theatre except to see some new play of Euripides" and H.B. Cotterill (*Ancient Greece*, p. 358) even suspects Socrates "of having a hand in some of these plays." Aristotle called Euripides the "most tragic of poets."

The divorce of art from philosophy, as also from religion and ritual, was a later development and, as we travel down the alleys of time to our own modern age, the estrangement between art and philosophy becomes wider than ever. By such a compartmentalization both branches have suffered and the central theme of both, which is the mystery of the Absolute, which both are to unravel, has become more and more forgotten and left behind.

Philosophy itself in turn tended to become analytical, and the first bifurcation of its scope took place quite early in the history of thought when Aristotle had to part company with his teacher Plato on the issue of the world of the intelligibles of the latter and the world of actualities or prime realities of the former. Ascending and descending dialectics, instead of being considered as applying to one and the same central notion of the Absolute, were understood to refer to two distinct realities. The Aristotelian tradition has had a more pronounced influence on later thought. If we therefore look upon Aristotle with a certain respect here in the matter of understanding the unitive secret of drama we should feel fully justified.

Aristotle's Definition Re-examined

Aristotle's definition which we have already quoted contains some significant phrases, which should not pass unnoticed. In the first place tragedy is said to *imitate* some original. According to Plato the original of this imitation is in the world of the Intelligibles. To Aristotle, on the other hand, the reality imitated is nearer at hand and right here below in the world of humans.

When we know that the whole zigzag course of Western philosophy represents the dialectical interplay between the two worlds of these twin yet rival philosophers, it is not hard to see how a central notion of the Absolute has merely got to be supplied by us, to see how vestiges of duality could be finally abolished by the unitive non-dual concept wherein the apparent conflict between the theories of the two philosophers could be effectively resolved.

We said simply that it is the Absolute that art imitates. The second phrase that concerns us in Aristotle's definition is what refers to the subject matter of Tragedy which should be "of high importance, complete and of a certain amplitude." What the three epithets are meant to indicate is not clear to a modern reader, but in the mind of Aristotle and to the minds of many of his contemporaries, they must have made more meaning than to us, to whom they are but pointers towards some unitive or central value in life which, according to what we have stated, cannot be anything other than what the Absolute represents.

The other hints thrown out in Aristotle's *Poetics* are his remarks: "A thing can be whole and yet lacking in amplitude," and again, referring to the "pattern" of a "fable" that should be given a correct tragic "disclosure," he indicates that it must have a "beginning," a "middle" and an "end." The beginning is to be recognized by the fact that there is no beginning before it, and the end by the fact that nothing follows or is to follow naturally by the very nature of the fable. The middle is where the complication is to be located and has to refer to both the others. All these requirements are easily understandable. What makes us suspect, however, that Aristotle had really in his mind a dialectically and not merely an organically conceived pattern for a true Tragedy, is brought to light when he stipulates that the "end" has to be the *opposite* of what constitutes the "beginning."

The third phrase of the definition which is of importance to us is the stipulation that tragedy should be "acted and not narrated." It is in the Self that action which is overt and action which is innate could exist together in a unitive, therefore living and tragic form, instead of being a second-hand reality of narration. A bound Prometheus can be a representative of such a Self and thus reveal those tragic absolutist traits that give dignity to Man.

Ambivalent Aspects of the Soul of Tragedy

In Tragedy, then, we see our own self with all the possibilities and probabilities of natural, legitimate or just action disclosing itself round it in a form that is full of the breath of life. To write a Tragedy in this sense, as the classical sages understood drama at its best, the self has first to be visualized in its own proper setting both in dialectical terms and in the context of the Absolute.

This was the reason why, in ancient India, in Sanskrit literature *nāṭaka* (drama) was the ultimate limit of poetic genius as enshrined in the adage *nāṭakāntam kavitvam* (poethood culminates in drama). When a child acts out, say an accident that he might have witnessed on the road, before he has learnt to describe it in the form of a narrative, he is really nearer to the original and greater than a mere narrative poet, and attains to a truer status as a dramatist, for action is a more direct expression of the self. He puts into it something of his inner sense of wonder and identifies himself unconsciously with what he acts. No pseudo art can find place in such a genuine stuff. What he means from his inside and what the action is meant to imitate in the world of actual happenings meet in the child, who, though helplessly dumb, is eloquent through art, even in spite of his omissions and errors.

Dramatic action is the meeting place of overt and inner action. These two classes of action really refer to two ambivalent aspects of the Absolute which meet in the human psyche or self. In drawing the difference between Comedy and Tragedy, Aristotle himself refers to these aspects when he writes of two kinds of characters in drama as follows: "This is the difference that marks Comedy from Tragedy: Comedy is inclined to imitate persons *below the level of the world*; Tragedy persons *above it.*" Evidently Platonic or hypostatic values are under reference here, when Aristotle makes the distinction between persons *above* and *below* the level of the world.

As with characters, actions may be similarly classified. When we keep in mind the secret of Dithyrambos which refers to the central figure of Dionysos, who in turn represents the Absolute Self, as we have already touched upon, and try to understand this ambivalent principle in the light of other sayings we have cited, such as the one which refers to the "blessing" of Dionysos as the *counterpart* of the "blessing of *bread*," and finally also that other enigma in which the God Dionysos himself is spoken of as being *"poured out in offering to the gods,"* the modern mind, given a little intuitive understanding or imagination, cannot fail to see the mystical doctrine that underlies this kind of allegorical language.

The Bhagavad Gita puts the paradox involved masterfully, when it states that one has to be able to see *action in inaction and inaction in action* to be called wise among men. Unitively understood in this way, it will be seen that elements of Romance and Tragedy meet and fuse into each other dialectically in any drama worth the name. As J.W. Krutch would put it, "Tragedy is essentially an expression, not of despair, but of the triumph over despair and of confidence in the value of human life." He adds elsewhere, "All works of art which deserve their name have a happy end. . . . It is a profession of faith and a sort of religion."

I.A. Richards in his *Principles of Literary Criticism* puts his finger on this very point of balancing counterparts in Tragedy when he writes:

> It is the relation between the two sets of impulses, pity and terror, which gives its specific character to Tragedy, and from their relation the peculiar poise of the tragic experience springs.[11]

The Common Criteria of both Romance and Tragedy

The pattern or scheme to which both Romance and Tragedy must conform to make them an elevating, serious, noble or sublime work of art, may first be centralized round the Personality of Man himself. The divine and the satanic are ambivalent aspects of human nature, with heaven and hell as worlds corresponding to each of these poles of life.

Satan is an immortal with the secret of double negation implicit in the human value he represents. The omniscient, omnipotent and omnipresent God or Zeus on high is also immortal, and belongs to the same contemplative context of double assertion. Between them there is a subtle reciprocity of relation as between the Absolute and the Relative. Satan himself could be considered very respectable because he represents the necessary counterpart of the free or contingent aspect of life.

In the more correct dialectics of pre-Christian thought, Pluto, and the Goddess Demeter with Persephone, represent the aspect of bread which is negative or necessary, while God Zeus brought up the vanguard of free divine values.

---

11. *Eight Great Tragedies*, Mentor, New York, p. 432.

Thoroughgoing Pagan dialectics prevailed before the new Gods of Olympus came into vogue and the central figure here was of Dionysos who was known to be the counterpart of bread as a blessing to life. He represented freedom.

Between the plus and minus poles of contemplative values we have to imagine an axis of graded intermediate values. Jacob's ladder upon which angels went up or down represents this axis in myth. This same myth has been modified in other similar myths of later origin, as for example, in Goethe's *Faust* where Powers of Nature ascend and descend and reach to each other's golden vessels filled with the waters of life. One who reads Dante or Milton will be able to discern these graded value-worlds described with great minuteness of detail, and in Goethe's *Faust*, where we have a drama which conforms to the required pattern in its structure and amplitude, we have several sub-human and supra-human worlds introduced. *Faust* again proves that the worst tragedy in a horizontal or outer sense could be the sublimest of happy romances viewed vertically. The middle of the play is punctuated by the worst imaginable of tragic events, but at the end of the second part of *Faust* full amends are made in this matter, which is so evident in the words of her who on earth was called Gretchen, but glorified above as Marguerite:

O Mary, hear me!
From realms supernal
Of light eternal
Incline thy countenance upon my bliss!
My loved, my lover,
His trials over
In yonder world returns to me in this.

— Tr. H.B. Cotterill

A Common Structural Scheme for Romance and Tragedy

A central Self or Soul caught between heaven and earth is pictured in both Romance and Tragedy. The dominant note of both is a supreme bliss of happiness when the Soul or Self is able to transcend horizontal forces that intervene disastrously in the middle of the play.

If we take the case of Othello we see him a changed man after he becomes aware of the innocence of Desdemona. He is no more a murderer. His heroism as a soldier was interrupted by suspicion, but he soon caught up with his own nature and rose to tragic stature. His tragic exaltation gives him a new status, although the end aspect of the pattern of the play has been made very abrupt. The hero transcends pleasure and pain and attains a degree of exalted bliss that has an absolute character when playing on the words "kiss" and "kill," as if they were interchangeable terms. He stabs himself saying: "Killing myself die upon a kiss."[12]

In the case of *Alcestis*, as we have already seen, the vertical and horizontal aspects of the structure of the play are perfectly and symmetrically conceived. Coming back to life is the core of vertical action, and dying to make the King Admetus, her consort, the most unhappy man, belongs to the dualistic context of the horizontal amplitude of the play. The dualistic and unitive attitudes are juxtaposed cleverly by Euripides himself when he makes Admetus say: "Those who are about to die are dead, and the dead are nothing," to which Herakles replies in a unitive spirit, "Men hold that to be and not to be are different things."[13]

In *Hernani* the double suicide marks the dualism of the horizontal, and the vertical amplitude is left merely suggested to the imagination of the reader or spectator. Elements of the vertical amplitude are present in the character of Doña Sol, as it were below the level of the world, and in the adventurous Hernani above it; and the flight of the two souls together, if it had been also acted out, would have given the play a more complete

12. V.ii.359.

13. *Seven Famous Greek Plays*, Alcestis: Modern Library, New York, p. 261.

structure and revealed the truly tragic heights which, as it is, are merely implicit rather than explicit. The words, "Let us depart in equal flight towards a better world" are perhaps the only ones which refer to the positive aspects of the vertical amplitude. Making allowances for differences of structure of this kind, we can therefore see how both Romance and Tragedy conform to the same basic pattern.

If we take the case of Kālidāsa's *Śākuntalam*, the structure reveals the same scheme of value references. Although she occupies the centre of the play like Alcestis, Śakuntalā scarcely speaks and the action is mostly the wrong done to her rather than anything she does herself. The element of wonder is brought in by a heavenly voice and she finally rises into the higher world by mere truthfulness to her own pure nature.

Nemesis and Katharsis Unitively Understood

When the structure of a play, whether Romance or Tragedy, is understood as having a beginning, a middle and an end, and, if we should grant also that the end has to have an opposite character to the beginning, then it is easy to concede that the middle is the seat of the complication or the conflict. When the conflict has an amplitude which lies along the horizontal axis we have the tragic phenomenon known as *nemesis*. When this is transcended through sublimation into a higher state of mind and the central hero, twin spirits, or heroine, as the case may be, avails of the sweet uses of adversity, we have the phenomenon known as *katharsis*. By the *rapport* between the onlooker and the actor *katharsis* works as a purifying influence on both. If the doctrine of vicarious suffering is to have any sense at all, it is in this way.

Affiliated to the context of wisdom, man is capable of transcending horizontal and mutually exclusive conflicts by a unitive and absolutist attitude whereby he feels happy at a higher level and thus solves even the worst problems that life can present. He outlives pain by transcending the worst outer or mechanistic circumstances. He lives in the golden mean of the middle way where the four different aspects of reality cancel themselves out into a neutrality which belongs to the Absolute.

These four aspects of reality are the virtual and the actual of the horizontal axis, and the negative and the positive of the vertical axis, in the scheme of the Absolute viewed as the supreme cosmological and psychological Person both subjectively and objectively. These terms have to be placed in their proper philosophical perspective to be grasped. Aesthetics has to be treated as part and parcel of a unitive and absolutist view of life. We shall not dare to enter into this task here, but content ourselves in the remaining portion of this essay with trying to distinguish the limbs or component parts of the structure of drama so as to justify and exemplify the generalizations we have made in the course of our discussion.

The Vertical Series of Worlds in Heroic Poetry

The highest role of poetry is where it fulfils the requirements of pure morality and religion, and culminates in revealing Man and the World of Man in the light of supreme Wisdom. Man is haunted by strange anxieties and fears. Despair and hope alternate in him minute after minute and stage after stage in life.

Doubts are of all grades and are his worst enemies. Man seeks with all his heart, whether consciously or unconsciously, to know the Beyond and how he has to attune himself with that great Beyond which is the Absolute in himself. Great epics of all great people and civilizations have given broad hints in this matter. The lasting popular interest in such works as those of a Homer, a Vālmīki or a Vyāsa are meant to feed and satisfy the eternal craving for wisdom in the heart of humanity. Here again it is around personalities called heroes who have some absolutist traits that the grand poems unravel in heroic metres the story concerning some heroic episode.

Great men and women with this stature, which is no other than that of the tragic character, are equally capable of great mistakes and great acts of nobility or bravery, and are presented in their proper living settings in epics so as to enable the reader to place his own Self or the Soul or the Personality of Man similarly within its proper setting. Freedom and necessity regulate their movements and actions from two opposing poles. Their struggles represent the normal and natural agony of the human spirit. Dante, Milton and Goethe have kept alive this tradition in literature and made their striking immortal contributions. Tennyson and others have written similar poetry of lasting appeal to the popular mind.

In every case a careful reader will be able to distinguish a vertical and a horizontal scale of values involved. There is an ascent and a descent. If this is not in cosmological terms it would be implied in psychological terms. Gods and men and the subhuman world come into dialectical interplay. Romance and Tragedy could be said to belong to the same context as heroic poetry, implying the same conflicts or trials of heroes. In Romance and Tragedy the conflict is only brought into greater relief and amplified, and the drama as a whole is built round the central conflict.

The Structure of Goethe's Faust

In Goethe's *Faust,* which has the structure of an epic as well as a tragedy, the various graded worlds of value begin with the lowest level, described by Faust himself as a "scene of swinish bestiality" where brawling and tipsy students drink and make merry in Auerbach's Cellar.

Next in the scale is the Witch's Kitchen which is meant to be subhuman and out of the actual world. It is a kind of underworld where Mephistopheles feels quite at home and in good company among the Meerkatzer — queer male and female ape forms — sitting stirring a witch's cauldron. Faust finds this world more disgusting than the one before. When the cauldron boils over,

"With a hocus pocus of incantations the witch who comes down the chimney from the flames sent up by the magic liquid in the cauldron, brews the magic draught which Faust drinks. He is then hurried away by Mephistopheles back into the world of Humanity."

After thus being transported from the bowels of the underworld of human values into the one of simple normal values, we have the whole of the main tragedy built round the simple home of a girl called Gretchen, who is to be glorified in the higher world later as Marguerite with, as we shall see, a spiritual status as high as Mary the Mother of God herself. The pathetic little tragedy in the human world is touching and simple, but only a miniature model of the world of human relations is presented here. Goethe is more interested in the vertical series of worlds and passes on to another higher world.

After Gretchen has sunk fainting to the ground, the wild and curious scenes of the *Walpurgisnacht* and the scene of Oberon's Wedding which has been called a kind of "after-dream" of the *Walpurgisnacht*, supply two other value-worlds of a graded order in the vertical scale above the scale of the simple human level. H.B. Cotterill has the following significant observation about the multiplicity of worlds, especially these two last superhuman worlds of values which Goethe has created:

> The connection of these scenes with the main action of the play has puzzled many critics, especially the curious intermezzo which follows the *Walpurgisnacht*, "the Golden Wedding of Oberon and Titania," a kind of dream vision, or rather nightmare, in which besides the fairies of Shakespeare's fairyland, besides will-o'-the-wisps and weather-cocks and shooting-stars, numerous authors, philosophers and artists and other characters appear, including Goethe himself as the *Welt-kind* (world-child).

And the same writer explains his own viewpoint further on when he writes on the relevancy of these scenes as follows:

> Although not written for the play, this intermezzo cannot be said to be superfluous, for the subject of *Faust* is one that admits of almost *any imaginative conception that is descriptive of the experiences of human nature in its quest for truth.*[14]

Puzzle for Critics

The puzzle of the critics arose because most of them simply thought a tragic end made a Tragedy. The dialectical scope of Tragedy with the peculiarities of structure and amplitude require a vertical series of worlds through which the spirit of man should pass before the triumphant end of Tragedy could be normally attained. The pure intellectual agony of a man aspiring for wisdom is the central theme of the *Faust*, and the path of such a progression has to have its course marked by intermediate stages of value-worlds, all of which have to lie on a scale which is vertical. The amplitude of a Tragedy has to move in a vertical scale of values before tragic or even romantic character could be given to any play.

To distinguish this vertical series of worlds in *Faust* we have first to mark the centre, which is represented by Gretchen's simple human world. This is the dialectical middle position where the pure inner and the practical, gross or mechanistic worlds of actual pleasure, come together. Even the noblest of characters, of whom *Faust* could be considered representative, have within themselves this common meeting-point of the pure and the gross aspects of life as an everlasting possibility. The human hero sometimes passes into the extraneous or non-spiritual aspect of life by sheer necessity. We have to distinguish the horizontal world of lust or pleasure which touches the vertical at some point or other in human nature and crosses it so as to make Tragedy. H.B. Cottorill himself is at first puzzled why Faust should have bestial experiences and a blood-stained hand before he is finally saved, and he pertinently remarks:

---

14. *The Faust Legend and Goethe's Faust*, Harrap, London, p. 98.

> Faust is (as so often is the case with noble and loveable men) open to assault at that point where, as nowhere else, the sensuous and ideal in our human nature seem to touch and coalesce.[15]

Mephistopheles surrounded by *witches* in the first part of *Faust* is the counterpart of himself, when in the second part he is made helpless by being surrounded by *angels* of heaven after Faust's grave was dug under his supervision. Protected from the double negation that Mephistopheles represents in himself, the spirit of Faust is able to rise and follow Marguerite into the world of wisdom and light. The Prologue in Heaven at the beginning of *Faust* belongs to the same world of values understood in rather Pythagorean terms of music of the spheres. Thus there is a series of vertical worlds in *Faust*, ranging from the Witch's Kitchen and Auerbach's Cellar, through the human one where the horizontal and vertical aspects of life coalesce or cross. Hypostatically, there is the world of the *Walpurgisnacht* and the fully hypostatic or ideological domain of the world in which the Golden Wedding of Oberon and Titania takes place.

Horizontal World of Values

Mythology and theology and secret doctrines of various kinds have made it easy for us to recognize the vertical series of values in life, but to tell exactly what differentiates the vertical from the horizontal requires philosophical insight.

Rousseau has a very striking sentence in which he refers to the two aspects which we have named vertical and horizontal here and in other essays. In the *Contrat Social* he wrote:

> As I meditated on the nature of man, it seemed that I discovered therein two distinct principles; one of them rose to the study of eternal verities, towards love, justice and true morality, to those regions of the world that the sage loves to contemplate; the other

15. *The Faust Legend and Goethe's Faust*, p. 92.

> lowered, rendered it slave to the senses, and of passions, which are its instruments, and was *thus opposed* to all that was suggested by the first principle.

Satan with a cloven hoof already belongs to the world of contemplation, because he represents in himself values that are natural to erring men. Satan as a rival to God must belong to the same contemplative, therefore vertical, though negative, context.

The distinction between Wagner, the laboratory assistant of Faust, and Faust himself would represent more correctly the two sets of values involving corresponding attitudes towards life. The contrast can be brought out by two short quotations from the *Faust* itself, rather than by descriptions of our own. The key to the difference is hinted at by Goethe in a very suitable way. Faust and Wagner go out for a walk and they both see a black poodle coming towards them. Faust says that he sees a trail of phosphorescence gleaming behind the poodle, but Wagner is unable to see this trail of light that belongs to life. He has a matter-of-fact, so-called modern scientific attitude to life which admits no contemplative elements. Therefore the world that he sees is different from the vertical world in which contemplative values lie. Faust's attitude is portrayed as follows:

> For in each soul is born the rapture
> Of yearning upward and away.
> When o'er our heads, lost in the azure
> The lark sends down her thrilling lay,
> When o'er crags and pine-clad highlands
> The poising eagle slowly soars,
> And over plains and lakes and islands
> The crane sails by to other shores.

On hearing these words, Wagner exclaims:

> I've had myself at times an odd caprice
> But never such impulses as these.

The woods and fields *soon get intensely flat,*
And, as for flight – I never longed for that.
— *Cotterill's translation*

There is an insipid world of horizontal values which consists of the feast of pleasurable things spread out in the world. The pleasures, however, have no depth in them, and one gets a surfeit of them quickly, as implied in the italicized words "soon get intensely flat."

Bacchanalian Revelry and Concupiscence Distinguished

Man has been created by God to enjoy life in a legitimate manner. If every kind of enjoyable experience is to be tabooed as sin or belonging to the Devil, an insipid world of horizontal values would be all that is left. Bacchus represents the pagan concept of natural enjoyment before Christianity killed out the simple joys of existence. That God put Adam and Eve in a garden rather than in a desert would show that he meant them to enjoy themselves, but the present Christian obsession with sin is a doctrine in which the pendulum swings to another extreme as wrong as pagan excesses (if any).

Goethe was sometimes called "the last of the pagans" although his hero Faust is finally taken to a very orthodox heaven following in the footsteps of Marguerite who is a devout Christian. In the intermediate stages of the passage of the soul from sheer bestiality to tolerable or permissible pleasures, the subhuman is disgusting except to Mephistopheles and, as against this, the levels of enjoyment raised above the common level are dear to Faust but not to Mephistopheles. There is subtle dialectics to be noticed here in the reciprocity of ambivalent factors implied in the positive and the negative pleasures under reference. In the *Alcestis* of Euripides we have Herakles coming as a guest to the house of Admetus whose whole household is in mourning for the departed Alcestis. This demi-god Herakles, however, who stands between Zeus and Hades as it were, in spiritual status resembling Dionysos himself, gives himself to Bacchanalian feasting while all the others are mourning. This is a puzzle to the servant of the royal household who had to please the guests. This touch of Bacchus is purposely introduced into the context of mourning by Euripides, because the absolutist attitude transcends sorrow. Herakles enunciates the principle of his joyful attitude characteristically in this play, as follows:

> Mortals should think mortal thoughts.

and again:

> Count each day as it comes as life, and leave the rest to fortune.[16]

Enjoyment of life in a natural or god-given sense was within the limits of a good and full life. Even the Bhagavad Gita gives *kāma* (desire) the status of the Absolute when it states:

> I am Desire when not opposed to the right way of life.
> — VII.11

Śiva himself, although the king of renunciation, is often represented as in mad ecstasy, and drink is not altogether unassociated with him. Dionysos, as we have seen, while still a god, has been spoken of as a libation poured out to the gods. The joys of contemplative life include all legitimate joys of this world, and this is the reason why Faust, though aspiring for nothing less than the highest wisdom, has not left touch with the various worlds of enjoyment that came to him through the agency of Mephistopheles, whose only fault is of not attaining positive levels of value. It is the Wagnerian world which is to be avoided, but the graded Mephistophelian worlds brought to Faust are considered by Goethe as necessary stepping stones to his great work of self-salvation. Simple concupiscence and the ecstasy that naturally and legitimately belongs to a life lived fully, have thus to be distinguished.

16. *Seven Famous Greek Plays*, Modern Library, New York, p. 271.

Kālidāsa's Blending of Tragic and Romantic Elements

Kālidāsa's *Śākuntalam*, one of the world's literary masterpieces, provides a supreme example of a play where the edges and angularities of both Romantic and Tragic interests are rounded off and harmonized in the form of contemplative literature.

The very first verse of *Śākuntalam* gives us a key to the cosmology of the poet. He has a most comprehensive vision of the universe, which is shared by the other poets of the Golden Age of Sanskrit literature, like Daṇḍin, and even by Vyāsa in the Bhagavad Gita, where a vertical series of contemplative worlds belonging to the context of the unitive Absolute are enumerated:

> Earth, water, fire, air, sky, mind, reason also, and consciousness of individuality, thus here is divided My eightfold nature.
>
> This is the non-transcendental. Know the other to be My nature, which is transcendental, constituting life, Arjuna, by which the phenomenal world is sustained.[17]

Heaven and earth do not belong to two dualistically conceived levels of reality here, but the ego on the one hand, which represents the aspiring soul in man, and the earth which is a reality in an everyday ontological sense, are strung together with other intermediate value-factors such as water, fire, air, sky, mind and reason, all of which counted make eight entities or value-factors representing the whole range of hypostatic or hierophantic value-systems of fundamental human interest. The Absolute itself knows no trace of duality when finally understood according to the cosmology and psychology developed in the Gita. The Sanskrit poets adhered to this scheme, with slight variations as between individual poets, as the family resemblance between the cosmology of a Daṇḍin and a Kālidāsa amply reveals to the student.

It is in Kālidāsa's other great drama *Vikramorvaśīyam* that the

17. Gita, VII.4-5.

purity of the scheme becomes better still exemplified. The scenes in this play are laid not merely in the world of humans, but in all the three value levels. Urvaśī, the heroine, belongs to heaven, but falls in love with a mortal king by a strange conspiracy of natural circumstances. Like the Forsaken Merman of Mathew Arnold, Urvaśī is lost again for the mortal king, who wanders in extreme pangs of separation but sees, through his pangs, in the human world itself, intimations of the world of immortality, revealed as the beauty of the neck of a swan or the voice of a *koel* (the Indian cuckoo). Heaven and earth seem blended to his contemplative vision. Urvaśī herself, through the anger of the gods, has to be born and pass her life for some time as a simple herb lost in a neglected part of a mountain valley.

Thus the vertical scale of values deftly fingered by the poetic genius of a Kālidāsa ranges from the world of medicinal herbs and gems to the world of the gods of *svarga* (Heaven) with all its pleasures and luxuries. The horizontal factors are hardly brought in, so that only a contemplative can fully enjoy the play as it moves purely within the amplitude of the vertical axis.

Kālidāsa's *Kumārasambhavam* (The Birth of the War-God), though an epic poem, reveals in its opening verses the same scheme and pattern of the world of values. The earth is there compared to a milch cow yielding precious stones and healing herbs under the presiding superintendence of Mount Meru, the Olympus of the Indian contemplative context. The Himalaya (Abode of Snow), where Śiva and Pārvatī live, constitutes the other pole. Between these two poles the epic moves in its majestic strains, combining romantic and tragic elements, particularly in the scene where Kāma (Eros) is turned to ashes by the fiery gaze of the central eye of Śiva, while pure Love triumphs to unite him with Pārvatī.

Poetic or Divine Justice

All religions have what corresponds to a heaven above or hell below. The descriptions might have variations with elements of wine or women dominant or recessive as the case may be. Joining these two poles of value-worlds, there is a scale upon which, as Goethe imagined, angels or powers of nature ascend or descend and reach to each other's golden vessels filled with the waters of life. Such a vertical axis has its positive and negative aspects. All below the level of earth, as Aristotle would say, consists of comic values corresponding to bread, and there is a positive aspect of the same where true tragic values reside and where the sheer joy of divine blessing is said to be offered to the gods as a libation of wine.

The horizontal element that outer circumstances might bring to bear on this pure vertical movement of life would at once spell disaster, great or small, gruesomely tragic in its inexorable *nemesis* of pity and fear or in a sense that forces of evil are transcended through *katharsis*. The expiation comes from experience which is inner, outer, or both.

In the case of Faust, he had to learn the hard way through the worst of tragic developments, but hope of rebirth into a pure life was not shut against him. A Beatrice or a Marguerite comes down from the higher pole of light to lead the erring soul of man. The sinner who listened to the voice of the principle of negation is again saved by being united with the positive light of wisdom which is the most potent factor in the process of self-salvation open to man.

Such are some of the broad lines along which poetic and divine justice work without contradiction. The pagan and the Christian, the Believer and the Kaffir, have the same fundamental factors of divine or poetic justice to guide their destinies. To swerve from the vertical axis of one's own *dharma* or natural sequential action develops Tragedy, and catching up with purer vertical values spells the transcending of evil and a rebirth, redemption or resurrection as in the case of a pagan Dionysos or a Christian Son of God. The *Rāmāyaṇa* and the *Mahābhārata* as told by Vālmīki and Vyāsa respectively, have the same frame of reference within which divine or poetic justice may be said to live.

All virtues and worthwhile values in life belong to the vertical axis of life, viewed both cosmologically and psychologically, and as both transcendent and immanent. Poets and seers have had the common task of interpreting this verity in various ways which we have tried to reduce into a schematic language like that of a mathematical graph. It is not meant to be a rival doctrine, but intended merely to help us to appreciate spirituality in more open terms than hitherto.

It is the Absolute which is the Self in which we find all human values strung vertically "as pearls on a string," as the *Gītā* says. The Muse has to finger all the strings of her lyre to make Romance or Tragedy succeed.

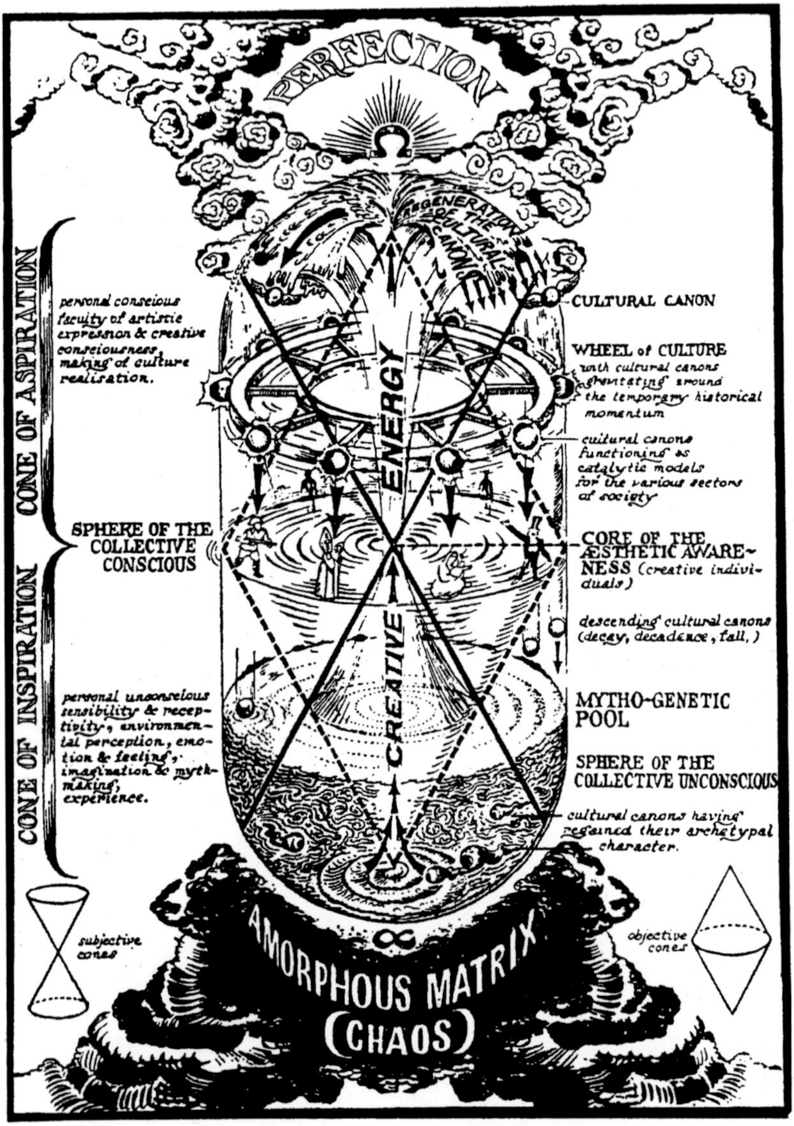

Courtesy: Jean Letschert, a French artist

4

Man-Woman Dialectics: I

A BEAUTIFUL woman is a problem to herself and society, and a strong and brave man likewise needs to control himself or be kept within bounds. Many men for one woman, and many women for one man are equally vexatious to both parties concerned. An Ares-Aphrodite (Mars-Venus) dialectics is implied in the saying "None but the brave deserves the fair." The world of rumour and of honour intervenes between the two poles involved here, wherein seeds of unforeseen tragedy can germinate quickly in human affairs. An overgenerous man in a right society or a misfit woman in a wrong one can spell disaster. Four-cornered or triangular relational situations can develop which often breed ugly dramas in slums and cities. Sex promiscuity becomes insipid or absurd. Crime and delinquency find a fertile hotbed in such an atmosphere.

Seen from the domestic angle a nice-looking couple at a party might be ill matched, while what is lost in public life may be a gain in favour of private life. A "cock-sure" woman and a "hen-sure" husband, as D.H. Lawrence would distinguish some modern types, often compromise the case of both. In such cases companionship is a double pain rather than the twice-blest joy it should be. An ugly man might seem attractive to a fair woman. A subtle dialectical reciprocity is operative here. Some men with a woman's reason or some women with a man's emotion or passion can introduce by wrong combination of factors, further complications into the matter of Man-Woman Dialectics.

Factors still more subtle are implicit in Man-Woman Dialectics which we have to examine in the light of Destiny, Fate or Providence as revealed in the great classical tragedies of Euripides and Sophocles, who have lavished much wisdom on this aspect of human life. Even excess of chastity or generosity, in spite of great precautions, can be disastrous, as in *Oedipus the King, The Women of Trachis* or *Hippolytus*. The conflict of life and death itself is evidenced as Tragedy. Absolute wisdom has to face the unexpected. Remaining itself a mystery, it requires the dialectical approach which alone can cut the knot with its two-edged sword which so often figures symbolically in the writings of the classical dramatists. The role of the gods who enter into rival interests has to be kept in mind if we are not to miss the light on Man-Woman Dialectics that these great works shed on the secrets of human life irrespective of time or clime. A frustrated woman can go mad herself or drive others mad. A man who consciously or unconsciously violates delicate laws here can bring down disaster on himself and the whole country.

Outward love and inward hate as between couples living under the same family roof, violating subtle laws of eugenics, can adversely affect generations to come. Romance often has a tragic core. It calls for the highest type of dialectical wisdom to exercise discretion even in everyday problems such as community living or co-education. Healthy relations may degenerate quickly into promiscuous absurdity involving again the law of double loss or gain.

Such are some of the implications of the subject of Man-Woman Dialectics which we shall here stop a while to consider, having duly explained the terms, the axes of reference, and the methodology generally of this way of approach, which insists on discussing the interests of the sexes together and unitively instead of disjunctly, one at the expense of the other, as has more often been done by such writers as Nietzsche and Schopenhauer. Not "Man and Woman" but "Man-Woman" is our formula here. In this first part of our study we shall examine generalities, reserving more specific aspects of the subject for the second part.

The Absolutist Background

Sex relations considered mechanistically or unilaterally outside the context of dialectics that properly belongs to the notion of the Absolute or has the Absolute as its normative principle, would not help human discretion to guide conduct intelligently. Even when a woman has to select her hat she has to look at herself and her hat alternately or together before she can make up her mind correctly. On the other hand, if a car should break down for want of a nut the dialectical approach would be absurd. Objective mechanistic reason may be or may not be exercised, and no inner contemplative or prayerful attitude will suffice by itself. Faith can move mountains only within the world of contemplation, to which the value called mountain need not be considered outside. The limits of the mechanistic reason and the point of its contact with the contemplative is a subtle philosophical question as between the "actual" and the "perceptual," to which problem the Bhagavad Gita devotes a whole chapter (the XIIIth). Actuality and substantiality meet as Value in relation with the normative principle of the Absolute, and all happenings in human affairs, whether tragic or romantic, have to be fitted into the general context of the Absolute if they are to make any sense at all. Otherwise life would be only a silent mystery. It would yield no guiding principles for intelligent living. Dialectics is the two-edged sword of wisdom that cuts both ways the riddle of the paradox of life, and can resolve it, as has been often symbolically alluded to in the writings of the great classical masters of drama (e.g. *Electra* and *The Women of Trachis* of Sophocles).

Life consists of a central paradox. Life and death meet as it were from opposite sides each moment of the eternal present. In other words, the plus and minus of life are ever cancelling out into the neutrality of the Absolute. Man and woman are the main actors in life, who represent its two ambivalent limbs. When they meet horizontally as man and woman in the actual world of action, their creative energy expresses itself as living progeny, but when the plus and minus represented by each of the sexes dialectically or interchangeably meet in the world of vertical values, creativeness becomes sublimated into universalized forms of life-expression of various grades ranging from the role of a great ruler or a teacher of men, culminating in the pure worlds of Value in which theory and practice meet. This idea is quite familiar to classical writers, and Plato in his *Symposium* states in the words of Diotima to Socrates:

> Those whose creative instinct is physical have recourse to women, and show their love in this way, believing that by begetting children they can secure for themselves an immortal and blessed memory hereafter for ever; but there are some whose creative desire is of the soul and who conceive spiritually, not physically, the progeny which is of the nature of the soul to conceive and bring forth. If you ask what that progeny is, it is wisdom and virtue in general; of this all poets and such craftsmen as have found out some new thing may be said to be begetters; but by far the greatest and fairest branch of wisdom is that which is concerned with the due ordering of states and families whose name is moderation and justice.[1]

If drama is an epitome of life and man and woman are the chief actors therein, and if the plus and minus sides that they represent dialectically, though not actually always, are the forces that interact in the play under the rule of the three unities observed by classical dramatists, it is easy to concede how the notion of the Absolute lies always at the basis of the drama itself. In its action that is unravelled, drama only represents how the plus and the minus, the vertical and the horizontal, aspects of human life keep constantly cancelling themselves out in the eternal present or the

1. Plato, *The Symposium*, tr. W. Hamilton, Penguin, p. 90.

dialectical moment in which life must express itself. It is only in this philosophic sense that the closing words of that great play of Sophocles, *The Women of Trachis*, could be understood or justified. Hyllus, the son of Herakles, who is tragically bereaved of both parents for no intentional fault of theirs, sums up the import of the play as follows:

> Women of Trachis, you have leave to go,
> You have seen strange things,
> The awful hand of death, new shapes of woe,
> Uncounted sufferings;
> And all that you have seen
> Is God.

Fate, Providence, Dionysos, or the Spirit that survives Death or triumphs over it, are to be understood as notions representing Absolutist aspects, and drama in its best instances is used as a commentary on this central Absolute Value. A sense of moderation and justice is what the balanced notion of the Absolute is meant to instil into the mind of the wise or civilized man. The Golden mean in Man-Woman Dialectics is thus directly related to the wisdom of the Absolute.

The Horizontal Zone of Conflicts or Complications

The pretty girl in a village seeks a mate while many may seek her. Between the one and the many here there is an interplay of inner and outer life forces which could gather a momentum and attain tragic proportions ranging from a mere storm in a tea cup to a veritable siege of Troy. A duel fought, an angry father, or a clash of clans or castes are common occurrences that attend love episodes. When we do not think in terms of war or crime, between the question of the chastity of a woman and the chivalry of a man there is a horizontally spread zone over which, nurtured on gossip or rumour, an amorphous smokescreen covers human affairs. As with demand and supply, dialectics that belongs to this no man's land separating the sexes and their coming together, is masterfully touched upon by the author of the south Indian Tamil classic, the *Kural* of Tiruvalluvar of some 2000 years ago:

> Inside my body which is too weak to bear them, love and shame hang on either side of the pole of my life. — Verse 1163
>
> I cannot hide this disease, nor can I for shame reveal it to him who is its cause. — 1162
>
> To live in a village with no sympathetic people is painful indeed; but the pain of separation from the beloved one is more painful still. — 1158
>
> Will not the bracelets slipping from my arm proclaim the separation? — 1157
>
> My frail life hangs on the scandal that is afloat; it is indeed my luck that many are ignorant yet. — 1141

The same situation from the man's side is referred to as follows:

> Like that between the body and the soul is the love between me and this maiden. — 1122
>
> This maiden with her choice ornaments is like the soul living in (my) body; and when she is away it is as if the soul has left it. — 1124
>
> The village has helped me with its gossip; else it might have been hard for me to win this flower-eyed maid. — 1142
>
> Is the gossip of the village unfavourable to me? It makes me feel as if I already have what I have not yet won. — 1143
>
> My love has been strengthened by gossip; it might have lost its quality without it. — 1144

The suitable ambivalence and dialectics of the relation between the sexes, nourished or weakened by scandal, gossip or rumour, was well known to the contemplative vision of the antique Tamil saint as well as it is to any modern observer of human nature. Only a gentle flavour of dialectics is allowed by the saint to exude here. But when we come to the tragedies of Euripides and Sophocles the irony of Fate implied in Man-Woman Dialectics is ushered in, as it were, with a fanfare of trumpet blasts. Between one woman thinking of one man and many suitors for one Helen, there is a tragic no-man's-land that the brave and the fair have to traverse between them. Only then could Ares (Mars) rest his head on the gentle bosom of Aphrodite (Venus). The Greek tragedies offer us here a veritable panorama of possibilities.

The Vertical Axis

There are two kinds of morals with two different sources to which Henri Bergson has devoted a whole treatise (*The Two Sources of Morality and Religion*). This work is based on the dialectical tradition of pre-Socratic philosophers continued into the neo-Platonic school of, for example, Plotinus, and hence dialectical in its approach and absolutist in its outlook. If the world of gossip, rumour, honour, chastity or other social virtues, including justice, lie in one plane that may be named horizontal, there is the open dynamic world of freer moral values ranging vertically, whose norms depend on a different source altogether.

Closed and static morals have little in common with open and dynamic morals of spiritual life, although at the core of both one might contact the other differencelessly. Wisdom always insists that values relating to these two intersecting axes should be treated correctly as being independent of each other. Virtue, according to the *Nichomachean Ethics* of Aristotle, consists of being oneself fully and not interfering with others. Leaving extraneous matters well alone and minding one's own business is a rule observed even by the gods and goddesses of Greek mythology and religion. Although Artemis and Aphrodite sometimes make their votaries clash in their interests, the former goddess is made to say by Euripides in his *Hippolytus* the following significant words:

> For it is a law among the gods that none shall thwart another's will; we all renounce such interference.

The dialectical secret to be extracted here is that the gods act in the vertical plane only, while erring mortals, even when they are favoured by gods, might clash horizontally, for which the gods themselves disclaim any direct responsibility. Some element of the horizontal, whether in the form of a witch or an old gossip, is a necessary complicating factor in tragedy introducing a negative venom, or else it might be the haughty overbearing conduct of an Oedipus or a Theseus which brings disaster on their own heads.

What is important for us to generalize and state here as a law is that the horizontal aspect of life spells tragedy always, while the pure vertical is what gives a sublime and noble amplitude to the innate action implicit in life. In Man-Woman Dialectics we have to distinguish between the horizontal and vertical factors, as also the plus and minus, the male or female aspects of each case or situation, in order to aid our discretion or intelligence by which to guide our own lives.

The Two Aphrodites of Plato

If the goddess Artemis (Diana) is the dialectical counterpart of Aphrodite (Venus), whose rivalry was at the basis of the tragedy in which the over-generous man Hippolytus and the over-chaste woman Phaedra became involved by the mere gossip of an old nurse in a dire and double tragedy, a dialectically revalued version of the same mythology is found in Plato's *Symposium*, where there is reference to the two aspects involved.

The two rival goddesses, however, are brought together more unitively here with one name as the goddess of Love, Aphrodite, having two complementary, reciprocal and dialectically related aspects. The implications are evident in the following quotation which, read in the light of the two axes of reference that we have tried to explain, lays bare clearly the cross-strands of Man-Woman

Dialectics as clearly as we can reasonably expect at the present stage of our discussion:

> We all know that Aphrodite is inseparably linked with Love. If there were a single Aphrodite there would be a single Love, but as there are two Aphrodites, it follows that there must be two Loves as well. Now what are the two Aphrodites? One is the elder and is the daughter of Uranus (Heaven) and had no mother; her we call the Heavenly Aphrodite. The other is younger, the child of Zeus Dione, and is called Common (*Pandemos* — "of all the people") Aphrodite. It follows that the Love which is the partner of the latter should be called Common Love. I am not denying that we ought to praise all the gods, but our present business is to discover what are the respective characters of these two Loves. . . .[2]

An analysis of the difference between these two aspects of Love represented by the revised version of the mythology of Aphrodite by Plato and the deduction therefrom, constitutes a valuable classical text which supports the theory of Man-Woman Dialectics which we have developed so far and intend to pursue here. Plato enters into some of the subtler implications of the relation between the two Aphrodites as follows:

> There can be no doubt of the common nature of the Love which goes with Common Aphrodite; it is quite random in the effects which it produces, and it is this Love which the baser sort of men feel. Its marks are, first, that it is directed towards women quite as much as young men; second, that in either case it is physical rather than spiritual; third, that it prefers that its objects should be as unintelligent as possible, because its only aim is the satisfaction of its desires, and it takes no account of the manner in which this is achieved. That is why its effect is purely a matter of chance and quite often bad than good. In all this it partakes of the nature of its corresponding goddess, who is far younger than her heavenly counterpart, and who owes her birth

2. *Symposium*, Penguin, p. 45.

> to the conjunction of male and female. But the Heavenly Aphrodite to whom the other Love belongs, for one thing, has no female strain in her, but springs entirely from the male, and for another, is older and consequently free from wantonness. Hence those who are inspired by this Love are attracted towards the male sex and value it as being naturally the stronger and more intelligent.[3]

Diana or Artemis and Venus or Aphrodite hate each other, the former because the latter is not in favour of virginity. She herself (in Euripides' *Hippolytus*) explains her own distinction when she refers to her rival:

> as that pernicious goddess
> Whom myself and all to whom virginity is dear
> Particularly abhor . . . etc.

While likewise in the beginning of the same play, Aphrodite in her turn, is made to say,

> Hippolytus, by holy Pittheus taught
> . . . loathes the genial bed
> Nor to the sacred nuptial yoke will bow.

Diana the Huntress would represent the vertical positive principle in Man-Woman Dialectics, while Venus her rival would represent the negative aspect of the same. In the revalued version that Plato presents in the *Symposium* that we have quoted above, instead of being treated disjunctly, the roles of the two rival goddesses are brought under one and the same aegis of a unitive Aphrodite with a two-sided role. This revaluation of mythology in more unitive terms is recognized by scholars to be Plato's own original contribution to this delicate subject of Man-Woman Dialectics. Instead of rivalry, a dialectically conceived reciprocity is here substituted. The Common Aphrodite spreads her influence into the domain of horizontal values in life because of her interest in

3. *Symposium*, pp. 46-47.

progeny, and hence she is of bisexual origin, while the Heavenly Aphrodite is unisexual in her own origin which is given for purposes of recognition, the label of "male." Plato could have named this aspect as Androgynous, as well known in the Śiva myth of the Indian context, to be perfectly fair to both the sexes. The two Aphrodites, whether called male or male-and-female in origin, lie in the vertical scale of values because of the divine status they enjoy as sisters.

The Framework and Structure of Man-Woman Dialectics

Here a few generalizations may be permissible. In the first place we have to keep in mind that dialectical reasoning lives and moves only in the contemplative world of inner values whether moral or spiritual. Mechanistic thought which is called "objective" or "positive" is outside its scope although it has its own *raison d'être* in the world of actualities. Even within the world of contemplative values there is a framework within whose walls dialectics can operate according to its own method. Harmony, moderation, beauty, justice, equality or sameness established between dichotomous or ambivalent tendencies spells felicity, while excesses whether overt or innate when out of balance or in violation of the laws of subtle dialectical proportion, spells tragedy from a most unexpected quarter. Wisdom finds in the field of Man-Woman Dialectics a domain to exercise itself to great advantage for human beings.

We could attempt two further generalizations here. There is a horizontal axis which admits of dual rival elements which is the zone of all conflicts and complications, and secondly there is a pure vertical line in which all duality becomes resolved in unitive terms. Thirdly there is a tendency for a polarity to develop as between the positive and negative aspects of the vertical scale itself. If we should for convenience call the positive vertical the male principle and the negative vertical the female principle or factor, the difference or intensity of the polarity or ambivalence could vary in life as between a Mars and a Venus, as the Epicurean philosopher Lucretius (98-54 BCE) conceived dialectically the male god of war and the goddess of love in his poems. This version admitted sex dualism fully. In Aphrodite and Artemis of Greek myth transmitted as Venus and Diana through Latin, the goddesses were brought under a more unitive heading under a single female symbol of divinity though conceived as rivals. The polarity between the sexes is still recognized here. In the hands of Plato the two aspects receive a more unitive philosophical treatment although the asymmetry still persists as between the two Aphrodites. Within the frame of reference of the notion of the Absolute it is possible to examine more minutely and still more unitively the implications of the dialectical interplay of psycho-physical factors and the occasionalism implicit in the interaction of the dual sex factors.

Belonging as it does to no objective field of investigation, we have to support ourselves in any further scrutiny into this subtle domain of metaphysics, by means of time-honoured wisdom handed down by ancient civilizations where the validity is derived from popular consent of large populations for ages, rather than as based on experimental proof which cannot be resorted to easily in such a domain of knowledge. In ancient India and in China much popular wisdom is available, but for our purposes the gods and goddesses of the Greeks as understood by the great classical dramatists and philosophers lend themselves very readily for making the generalizations more explicit and to give them realistic flesh and blood. They supply the breeze in which dry-as-dust dialectics may gain a living and breathing status. We shall therefore quickly pass in review with the one-pointed eye of dialectics, about half a dozen Greek plays to fill in with meaningful content the elements of conflict, complication or resolution implied in this subtle question of Man-Woman Dialectics. A general familiarity with the plays under reference is assumed, although even for those who have not read the plays we have tried to indicate enough to enable the reader to discern the dialectics which is implicit in each case, as far as space permits.

A scheme of correlation of conflicting elements held together in the dialectics of Man-Woman as indicated in the diagram below may help to keep the component factors involved globally understood.

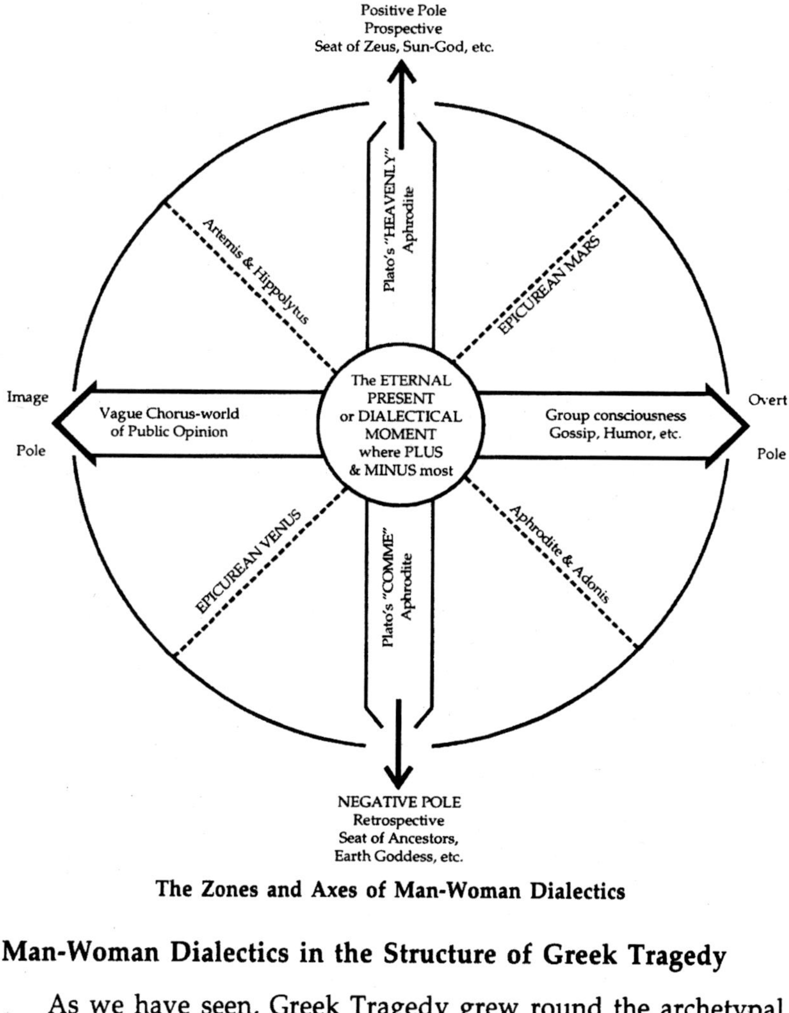

The Zones and Axes of Man-Woman Dialectics

Man-Woman Dialectics in the Structure of Greek Tragedy

As we have seen, Greek Tragedy grew round the archetypal figure of the enigmatic god Dionysos who combined in himself manly prowess and womanly grace, and represented in himself the process of eternal becoming in which life and death met and neutralized themselves in the notion of the Absolute. The androgynous god Śiva of the Indian soil represents the same Absolute as understood in the secret language of the *Tantraśāstra*. The frenzied women, who figured in the Bacchanalian revelry in which Dionysos was represented in the Eleusinian Mysteries as both dead and born again, give the cruel touch of negativism to the Absolute. Dionysos himself supplies the positive aspects of the vertical axis by his elusive and mysterious ways. The elements of Man-Woman Dialectics thus belong to the character of the god Dionysos himself, of which latter Greek drama, as we have elsewhere tried to explain, is merely a further elaboration and amplification. We shall pass in review about half a dozen plays of Sophocles and Euripides to clarify certain aspects of Man-Woman Dialectics, and try and remove thereby the obscurity that might still shroud the component elements and the modes of interaction of the conflicting factors that come into play.

1. THE BACCHANALS

Let us take as our first example *The Bacchanals* of Euripides, which is conceived along the purest of classical lines as a tragedy in the light of dialectics, and with Dionysos, himself of double origin, as the central figure as a character and as an invisible divinity, present throughout as the representative of the Absolute.

With the thunderbolt of Zeus burning the top of the "ash tree's heaven-reaching stem" on which Pentheus the ruler of the City-State of Thebes was raised by Dionysos, representing the positive male principle, and with the frenzied women of Thebes led by Agave the mother of Pentheus himself, bringing up the negative side, we have vertical aspects of the Man-Woman Dialectical situation clearly represented in all its tragic portent and wide amplitude.

Pentheus himself personifies the horizontal values cultivated in the closed and static conditions of the City of Thebes with standardized conventional morals and worship of tribal gods. The chorus is the voice of a public witness or opinion, swaying from one pole to the other, as the play unravels within its amplitude between the world of the high gods and the tender emotions and rivalry of the frenzied women of Thebes. The vertical movement of the frenzy in the mother makes her opaque to horizontal actualities, and Pentheus himself, when he by curiosity dons women's clothes to spy on the women in the forest, who were given to unconventional freedom outside the city at the instance of Dionysos, begins to abandon his own reason in favour of ill-understood vertical values. His own frenzied mother kills him and carries his head as a trophy thinking it to be that of a lion's cub. Memory and consciousness are reestablished in her too late.

In the case of the mother, the polarity as between the positive and the negative aspects in the vertical scale made an opaque gap in the middle for actualities. In the case of the son, his mistake was that he abandoned reason in favour of vertical values partially adopted out of curiosity and ill-understood in all their implications. The open, dynamic, absolute God thus triumphs over the relativistic, tribal, closed or static gods of Thebes. Thebes is thus spiritually and morally destroyed by the strange workings of Man-Woman Dialectics. Dionysos himself who is described in the play as combining masculine force and feminine grace, represents the neutral or androgynous principle of the Absolute which is both positive and negative at once. Pentheus' fall was in his inability to see his mother in the frenzied women generally, and the fault of Agave, his mother, consisted in her not being able to recognize her own son in her moment of frenzy. This is how the vertical and the horizontal, when they fail to be distinguished from each other by persons male or female, cross to form the substance of tragedy. The understanding of the Absolute as higher than all gods becomes the saving factor, if it does not come too late, in this play.

Some of the significant expressions found in the play which have bearing on what we have summed up above would tend to show how we should be justified in thinking that dialectics, and especially Man-Woman Dialectics as outlined in this essay, was at the back of the mind of the great classical tragedians themselves.

When Dionysos has done his work on the spirit of Pentheus, he says to the women:

> bereave him first of sense;
> yet be his frenzy slight; this man is in our net.

The state into which Pentheus himself has fallen with the error of duality implicit in it, is described in his own words:

> Ha! now indeed two suns I seem to see,
> A double Thebes, two seven-gated cities. . . .

Pentheus is still able to realize even in his partially confused state that

> by force we conquer not these women.

The black and terrible Kālī-principle roused in his mother in mystical frenzy in the name of the absolutist God, is described in the words of the Messenger who reports the tragic event of the mother killing her own son, as follows:

> She foaming at the mouth, her rolling eyeballs
> Whirling round, in her unreasoning reason,
> By Bacchus all possessed knew, heeded not.

In spite of the son's fondling the cheek of the mother and appealing for mercy,

> She caught him in her arms, seized his right hand
> And with her feet set on his shrinking side,
> Tore out the shoulder — not with her own strength;
> The god made easy that too cruel deed.

It is significant also to note that, in the Messenger's words, the other women of the party, including two of Pentheus' sisters

> Tossed wildly to and fro lost Pentheus' limbs,
> The trunk lay far aloof, 'neath the rough rocks
> Part, part amidst the forest's thick strewn leaves,
> Not easy to be found.

The grandfather of Pentheus, father of Agave, who comes on the scene at the last stage, insists on repeating the same description of the horizontal scattering of the body of Pentheus with a touch of unrealistic mystery in it which we should not miss if we are to take note of the dialectical scheme in the author's mind in the structure of the play. Old Cadmus, while Pentheus' body is brought in, refers to it characteristically as follows:

> The body with long and weary search
> I found at length in one Cithaeron's glens;
> Thus torn, not lying in one place, but wide
> Scattered amid the dark and tangled thicket.
> — Extracts from Wodhull's tr. of
> *The Bacchanals*

The mystical language of a symbolic ritualistic origin is reflected here and the dialectical frame of reference is unmistakably evident not only here but in various passages of Euripides and Sophocles in their various other well-known compositions. We have lingered here a little long so as to avoid entering into textual details in examining in quick review some of the other plays in the light of the same dialectics with which we are concerned here.

2. PROMETHEUS BOUND

Here we have a play by Aeschylus in which the hero is a rock-fixed Titan who is against the high gods of heaven. Except for this slight asymmetrical position in favour of the negative aspect of the Absolute, Prometheus, like Dionysos, belongs to the vertical aspect in the dialectical scheme that we have outlined. The Zeus-principle would supply the positive aspect as the male, and Mother Earth on whom Prometheus relies so much would represent the negative or female aspect in the scheme adopted here. The punishment of Prometheus originates in Zeus himself, but favour comes to him from the other pole to which as the feminine element, he appeals at the end as his very last words:

O Mother Earth all honoured,
O air revolving thy light,
A common boon unto all,
Behold what wrongs I endure.

The Agony of Prometheus is placed between the Man in Zeus and the Woman in Mother Earth. The plan even of this simple tragedy conforms thus to the general scheme of Man-Woman Dialectics.

3. ALCESTIS

In this play of Euripides the pure vertical values adhere to the character of the heroine herself. Admetus, her husband, for whose sake she gives up her own life, is also an honest man, not only virtuous in himself but having social virtues in addition, as shown by the way he received Herakles even when in mourning. The plus and minus represented by Admetus and Alcestis are dialectically brought together unitively by the help of Herakles who represents the Dionysos principle in himself.

4. OEDIPUS THE KING, OEDIPUS AT COLONUS, AND ANTIGONE

These plays by Sophocles, though not strictly a trilogy, can be examined together. They represent Fate as an Absolute Value as it works out its end tragically through two successive generations. Fate itself with a central irony or paradox implied in it, is the vertical Absolute principle in all the plays. Oedipus in his person in the first play, as the successful and popular ruler of his state, represents the horizontal values, while being innocent of the vertical invisible hand of Fate.

The unconscious Man-Woman Dialectics works out as between mother and son. What was thought to be a horizontal relation between the man and the woman concerned, turns out to be vertical, and the implied conflict between the two attitudes is the cause of the double tragedy in which the woman kills herself and the king plucks his two eyes from their sockets.

In the next generation, as revealed in *Oedipus at Colonus* and in *Antigone,* the vertical and the horizontal aspects are conceived in perfect dialectical symmetry of twin male and twin female children. Oedipus, before he dies, is concerned about his daughters Antigone and Ismene more than about the boys, both of whom he curses as having the status of pretenders or usurpers. He calls the daughters to his presence by way of recognizing their spiritual value. The boys both belong to the positive and negative sides of the horizontal aspect of life and they cancel one another out as described by Sophocles himself as follows:

> His sons have fallen in one day by a twofold doom — each smitten by the other, each stained with a brother's blood.

In contrast to the conflicting male progeny of Oedipus, the female spiritual pair of sisters show a variation between them which lies along the vertical scale of personal values. A quadrangular dialectical interplay of interests is interwoven by the author in which the two types of brothers and the two types of sisters are fated to work at conflicting cross-purposes. Secrets of Man-Woman Dialectics conflicting horizontally, yet complementary vertically, are masterfully depicted and worked out delicately by this master dramatist of antiquity. Ismene, the negative vertical type, complementing the positive vertical type in Antigone, her sister, refers to themselves as "we two left alone helpless" against public law under their uncle Creon's strict rule, after Oedipus' death. Ismene teaches caution to rash-minded Antigone, who insists on giving a decent burial to her brother who was condemned by the uncle to have no funeral honours for his seditious attitude to the state. When none dared to transgress the law, Antigone, though single and deserted by her own sister, honours the brother's grave.

The pure or vertical nature of the devotion of Antigone to her brother is argued for dialectically by Antigone herself as follows:

> Never had I been a mother of children, or if a husband had been mouldering in death, would I have taken this task upon me in the city's despite? What law ye ask, is my warrant for that word? The husband lost, another might have been found, and child from another to replace the first born, but father and mother hidden with Hades, no brother's life could ever bloom for me again.[4]

The implications of the two axes with their vertical and horizontal components, each with its own positive and negative aspects, represented by the two daughters and the two rival sons, is made still more explicit by Sophocles in his second play *Oedipus at Colonus*. Oedipus is here no more a repenting sinner, but saying "I am a holy man"[5] himself becomes a truer representative of the silent and neutral Absolute. Before he dies he is able to predict his fate without the help of oracles. He is particular to die away from all near and dear to him in any relativistic context. King Theseus of Athens alone as a fellow absolutist is taken into confidence in his last days.

The implied conflict between the values represented by the sons on the one hand and the daughters on the other, is expressed categorically when Oedipus disowns vehemently both his sons and claims kinship with his daughters, saying significantly about the sons to one of them, and ignoring apparent sex:

> You banished me. . . .
> But I had daughters

4. *Seven Famous Greek Plays*, Modern Library, New York, p. 271.
5. Sophocles, *The Theban Plays*, Penguin, p. 79.

Whose never-failing care has nursed my life.
They are my sons; you are some other man's.[6]

The curse pronounced on one of the two sons, Polynices, in the same context proves that dialectics is quite explicitly in the mind of the poet when he writes:

May you in dying kill your banisher
And killing, die by him who shares your blood.[7]

The delicate dialectical distinction between the two sisters is to be read more between the lines when Ismene says, after Oedipus' death:

O that I could lie
In death beside him, and not to live
The life that will be mine.

Antigone strikes the more positive note based on a double negation when she says under the same bereavement:

I never knew how great the loss could be
Even of sadness: there was a sort of joy
In sorrow when he was on my side.[8]

5. ELECTRA

In this play by Sophocles the same vertical variation as between Electra who is positive and her sister Chrysothemis who is too negative, both daughters of Agamemnon, are studied in contrast. His wife Clytemnestra lived illegitimately with another man when the hero Agamemnon returned from Troy. The usurper conspired with Clytemnestra and killed him. Electra and Chrysothemis were left in the father's house under Aegisthius the new husband. The gap between the two sisters, one of whom is too positive in the

6. Sophocles, *The Theban Plays*, pp. 112-13.
7. Ibid., p. 113.
8. Ibid., p. 122.

vertical scale, and therefore suffers for her independent ways, and which is in contrast with her sister who is on the mother's side condoning or conniving at the crime, is supplied by Orestes the son who, grown to full manhood elsewhere in hiding, with vertical virtue and horizontal prowess harmonized in his person, returns, and kills both his mother and her partner Aegisthius.

Aegisthius' confusion at the end of the play before his death at the hands of Orestes is significant. Orestes, who represents the central Dionysiac principle standing for Absolute Fate, God or the Furies, is described characteristically by Orestes himself when he says to Aegisthius:

> Are you so blind
> You cannot tell the living from the dead?

Man-Woman Dialectics as between women representing the plus side in Electra and the minus side in Chrysothemis, is bridged by the Dionysiac principle representing absolute awareness in Orestes, as against the blindness of Aegisthius who was aware only of horizontal aspects of life and was caught between life and death values conceived dualistically.

6. HIPPOLYTUS

Nowhere in Greek Tragedy is Man-Woman Dialectics brought out with its pointed conflict more than in this play by Euripides. The woman concerned is Phaedra the young second wife of the great king Theseus, absent in other lands. By his first wife, Theseus had a son who hated women and marriage, and gave himself to sport as the votary of Artemis (Diana) the chaste goddess of the chaste. Phaedra was a votary of Aphrodite. We have already alluded to the polarity implicit as between the two divinities. Their rivalry necessarily made Phaedra and Hippolytus dialectical counterparts as between the two sexes, for Phaedra nourished intense yet secretly guarded love for her step-son. Both are depicted in the play as irreproachable characters and a perfect man and perfect woman both in chastity and virtue forming the dialectical counterparts of the vertical scale of values. An old nurse who pities her ward Phaedra in her love pangs and admires the purity and perfection of the grown up bachelor Hippolytus, happens to set fire to the situation by forming a horizontal link between the two. Tragedy has its stage set by now. Theseus returns to find his young wife dead, committed suicide with a letter in her hand imputing falsely incestuous advances by her step-son. The angry father banishes his son in spite of his pure innocence, and Hippolytus sustains mortal wounds in traversing a road leading out of the country in his carriage as it passes between the sea waves and the rocky coast. Too late, he is brought to his father Theseus, who finds him innocent.

Gods and humans mix freely in this play so that subtle dialectics can have full scope for development. The nurse who sets fire to the situation that was already made inflammable with tragic tension between the man and the woman concerned, is not an active conscious agent herself, but is merely interested in bringing the man and the woman together. She is the unconscious instrument of the force of necessity found in nature itself. The rival goddesses are helpless to interfere in the world of actualities because, as we have already noted, it is stated by Artemis herself that,

> . . . It is a law among gods that none
> Shall thwart another's will; we all renounce
> Such interference.

Divinities live and move only in the vertical plane each for each alone. The tragic element has to be introduced by the horizontal factor being supplied to ignite the situation. Artemis herself finds Hippolytus faultless when she says,

> It is thy generous soul
> Which hath destroyed thee.

Theseus the disillusioned father is able boldly to say:

> I by the gods was then deprived
> Of understanding.

To which the dying son replies equally boldly:

> On that in return
> Mankind could with their curses blast the gods.

The ignorance of Theseus, caused by the gods themselves, is thus the cause of tragedy here. It consisted in not knowing that when her reputation is at stake, the best of women may tell a lie and not even to save herself, but to die in double negation that sets right the Self with itself. Hippolytus, on the contrary, though finally dying, may be said to live in double glory which, like a double assertion, amounts to the same. The Absolute that Tragedy reveals is neither with the living nor with the dead; neither with men nor with women. It is at the core of life, in the eternal present or in the dialectical moment.

7. THE WOMEN OF TRACHIS

We have already made passing allusion to this masterpiece of Euripides. The vertical life interests in this play are to be shared between the devoted and generous women in it. Deianeira who had no keen interest in wedded life was chosen by Herakles, himself a god, as his companion in the last days of his labours on earth. She pined for her godly husband and excused him everything, even his affair with Princess Iole, King Eurytus' daughter brought to the palace of Herakles after his last victory as a captive nameless woman. The wife takes pity on the pretty and silent prisoner whom a messenger reveals to be "a famous name and famous beauty." Deianeira is willing to tolerate her and excuse her husband to the utmost extent possible to a woman, but then puts her hand right on the sore spot, beyond which the most discreet of women could not be expected to go. Even this limit is transcended by the wisdom of Deianeira. She even consents to put up with that ultimate position in which, as she puts it,

> But share the house with her, and share the husband,
> It is more than any woman can do . . .
> This is my fear,
> Herakles to be my *husband* but her *man*. . . .

As a woman capable of absolute discretion she finally reconciles herself even to this ultimate position out of regard for Herakles, as she herself tells the "Women of Trachis" who represent, as it were, the absolute conscience of womanhood. In spite of her personal discretion, however, tragedy is not averted. Herakles, whom she wants to keep within her influence, has to die because of her overconcern for him rather than from any rivalry with Iole. A magic mantle lovingly sent by the wife strangles the husband. She kills herself with the two-edged sword to avoid the situation that had developed with a cursing husband or a cursing son blaming her for unwittingly causing the death of Herakles through the effect of the mantle, which chokes him negatively through some godly spell in it. Absolutely innocent though she remained, relativistic factors from both poles of the vertical scale of life values killed her with its double edge. Caught between the anger of a son for the death unconsciously caused to his father, and the cursing of a husband she kills herself because of all-round misunderstanding, for which the gods alone were responsible. As the nurse describes the scene,

> And there we found her with the two-edged sword
> Thrust through the centre of her heart. Her son
> Cried bitterly at what he saw; he knew
> Poor lad, it was his anger drove her to it.

Her motive for committing suicide, is put in her own words:

> Can any woman lose the precious name
> Of virtue in which she trusted, and still live
> Branded with shame?

8. MEDEA

We cannot find a better classical example of Man-Woman Dialectics than this outstanding play of Euripides, wherein Jason decides to marry the young princess of Corinth putting aside his older wife Medea and his two sons. To avenge her divorce and banishment she has recourse to the most extreme of measures, and in the actual words of the play in which the leader of the Chorus breaks the news first to the father of the sons tellingly:

> Thy sons are dead; slain by their own mother's hand.

According to the poetic justice of Euripides, instead of suffering punishment for this slaughter of her own children, she is made to appear in the final scene as a divinity herself seated on a dragon-chariot. The pithy repartee between Jason and Medea is glorified, and gloating over the bodies of the two sons, touch the high watermark of Tragedy beyond which it cannot possibly be strained. Two examples of the kind of exchanges between them will help to reveal Man-Woman Dialectics at its worst:

> Jason: O my children, how vile a mother ye have found!
> Medea: My sons, your father's feeble lust has been your ruin.

and again later:

> Jason: O my dear, dear children!
> Medea: Dear to their mother, not to thee.
> Jason: And yet thou didst slay them?
> Medea: Yea, to vex thy heart.

Although Medea killed her children, her husband Jason had a full share, morally, in their death. Dialectically viewed in the light of Absolute Justice which ignores results or motives having their origin in the horizontal world of brute circumstances or events, both Jason and Medea are equally to blame for the tragedy.

It is true that tragedy could have been avoided if they had

not loved with such wrong intensity. The horizontal elements in the characters both of Jason and Medea cancelled themselves out in the neutral culmination of the tragedy, which, when viewed with reference to the vertical scale of values, leaves only the gods to blame. The terrible woman who can kill her own children is only the dialectical counterpart of a lustful man who reaches out to false horizontal values. The duality introduced by the excess of glory on one hand breeds the negative love of death for its own sake on the other. Man-Woman Dialectics thus cancel themselves out in the neutrality of the Absolute.

5

Man-Woman Dialectics: II

MAN-WOMAN Dialectics depends primarily on the recognition of the subtle inversion implicit between the sexes. One has to be familiar with the scheme of the Absolute with its proper methodological and epistemological frame of reference and the two principal axes of correlation of value factors,[1] to be able to see clearly how the component conflicting or complementary counterparts in male or female enter into living relationships in the actual drama of life.

The perspective as viewed from the side of man would present a totally different colour from what is presented from the woman's view. The two points of view can be treated disjunctly or unitively.

Criminal psychology is already familiar with love triangles involved in dramas of jealousy, which the front pages of daily newspapers display to the discredit of human nature. Even when Man-Woman Dialectics is conceived more correctly as bipolar, varying degrees of unitive treatment are possible as between dualism and non-duality. The question of the equality of the sexes can be approached quantitatively or mechanistically, yielding quite other conclusions from what a dialectical treatment would bring. When overt equality is secured, the innate relation of harmony between the sexes can still remain violated. Instead of being equal and opposite factors, male and female should be treated as dialectical counterparts to justly balance the delicate relationship involved in the best instances of conjugal love.

---

1. See chart on p. 81.

The taming of the shrew is perhaps as difficult a problem as taking the side of Xantippe against Socrates. Medea, who went to the extent of killing her own children to spite Jason, had her own justification, although not within the purview of mere common sense. Poetic justice of Euripides favoured her. To understand problems from the woman's side requires greater dialectical insight than to appreciate the more formal and logical standpoint of the man concerned. The woman tends to be more personal, synthetic, subjective and real. She excels man in the emotional and relational sphere, while it is with more theoretical, logical abstractions, supported by passion for action, that man often tries to overpower the woman in vain. Her silence becomes at times more eloquent than all his ravings. Her negative absolutism can put the crown on a tragic circumstance. The soul of womanhood can reveal sublime heights of absolutist value in life.

In the first part of this essay, theoretical generalities have roughly been covered. We shall pass on here to the more specific or actual aspects viewed especially from the side of negative absolutism.

Dialectical Equality of the Sexes

The slogan of the French Revolution had Equality as its central concept. The absolutist derivation of this concept has, however, been long overlaid and forgotten. When a modern man thinks of the equality of the sexes which is a corollary of the principle of the Equality of Mankind in the name of the Absolute, he tends to do so in terms of actual or mechanistic equality or at best explains this further by reference to vaguer notions such as equality of opportunity. For its full significance, however, we have to view it from another angle altogether. If we are prepared to admit that Greek tragedies are not mere crime stories in the modern sense, but contains deeper secrets from the minds of the wise men of antiquity who wrote them, the all-important difference between a merely quantitative and mechanistic view and the living, real, qualitative and vertical view of life factors, becomes amply evident. Reality can be viewed either in mere cross-section, or longitudinally giving full scope to the process of flux and becoming which is life itself in its eternal creative expression.

The analogy of the dragon has been employed to express this latter way of appraising reality. The head of the dragon vomitting smoke or fire would be the dialectical counterpart of the tail which is the other balancing and relational pole in the living situation which it is meant to represent in the mythological symbol. Dialectical equality of the sexes thus gains quite another significance from the mere cross-section view which the modern mind has been taking, although such a view is good so far as it goes, and is quite in keeping with the heritage of an age of science. When dialectics itself becomes raised to the status of a science, there will be nothing repugnant to the dignity of modernism to include this longitudinal view of life treated as a living process of becoming. Man, woman and child here have an integrated and unitive relationship. Like light and darkness, man and woman can then be looked upon as reciprocal counterparts in a situation in which both are involved, though belonging to poles that exclude each other.

Male and Female Versions of Absolutism

Zeus with his thunderbolt is an awe-inspiring god. Likewise, Rudra and Vīrabhadra are meant to be terrible aspects of Śiva in the Indian context. The feminine counterpart of the same is Kālī, the personification of all-devouring Time. Anyone who has approached a woman near enough will concede easily that the seemingly weaker or gentler sex can hide behind her sweet charms some deeper trait made of sterner stuff.

This dimension in women is not revealed ordinarily on a background of everyday life; but it is thrown into striking relief when something near and dear to the woman's soul is touched. The lioness with her cubs is more terrible than the male of the species. When involved in love, the girl of sweet sixteen can brazen herself, forgetting her whole background. Tragic situations astonishingly set off the negatively absolutist stuff lying buried within the apparently docile submissiveness of womanhood. Frustrated affection can drive the one-pointed bipolar relation as between a man and a woman to the point of madness which over-reaches the limits of ordinary reason.

The case of Medea and Jason, which we have examined in some detail already, brings the counterparts concerned into correct and symmetrical relief.

Medea may be said to have attained to the white heat of absolutism possible to womanhood, and this must be the reason why Euripides does not hesitate to give her a divine status in the last scene where, over the home and hearth where her two children were killed by her own sword, she is represented as standing in a celestial chariot beyond the reach of the revenge of Jason. She gives expression to what could be taken to represent the content of that negative absolutism to which the most heroic of women alone could rise. As a hero, Jason himself is not without a touch of absolutism, but the male version here cannot be said to be of the highest order of which man is capable. Sublimer heights of masculine absolutism are represented in other plays both ancient and modern. Heroism finally gets sublimated in terms of self-realization which goes beyond all utilitarian human values. Man and woman attain to their highest fulfilment here when the positive and negative aspects of the Absolute coincide as the most central of values in life.

Sex Divergency and Dimorphism

The physiological differences between the sexes have been objectively studied. Some generalizations have been arrived at which tends to reveal that exceptions and rules are not so easy to separate. Some men are women and vice versa. The overlapping of common traits becomes all the more pronounced as inner zones of the personality are attained. Instead of differences which lie along the horizontal axis of values, we come to see, as we delve into psychic factors, that the more real differences between the sexes depend on a variation in the vertical scale.

The mutual attraction between the sexes which makes one appear pleasing to the eyes of the other, has no objective norm. To the eye of a philosopher like Schopenhauer, women generally are narrow-shouldered, short-legged and ugly. Baldheaded and bearded men who might seem repulsive to persons of the same sex, might prove favourite manly types in the world of women.

Standardized beauty is a misnomer. Preferences and partialities prevail in the appreciation of beauty, and it would not be quite easy, even for the judges in a beauty contest, to see Helen's beauty in an eye of Egypt. Such contests are repugnant to people of taste or training in the dialectical way. Freaks can excite curiosity but not admiration. A girl who is a "tomboy" and a boy who is a "sissie" have only nuisance value in boarding schools.

The polarity as between the sexes is not to be measured by so-called "objective" norms, but requires to be treated dialectically to lead to sensible generalizations. Women's clubs are known to have both masculine and feminine types who love to play the role of husband or wife, and the phenomenon of transvestism observable in both the sexes in modern life brings in a further complicating factor in the diagnosis of the traits that should properly belong to the sexes. No cut and dried differences should be expected, but only those ambivalent tendencies which are common yet specific to the two sex modalities to which the neutral Self may be said to be subject in our common human life here.

The Diagnosis of Sex Characteristics

Even when we make due allowances for the above dialectical requirements, from the commonsense point of view it would be safe to remark that women generally tend to be shy and like to avoid the public gaze. They feel at ease in the home where they love to retire, rather than be in the marketplace. Tears come more natural to women than to men, although women might excel in endurance and patience. The village girl is bound more to the locality than is the boy of similar age. Her reputation in the world of gossip, especially of women at the well-side, is no negligible factor to her. Questions of chastity, honour and reputation, wafted this way and that by that vague factor called rumour, can seriously disturb her peace. Good looks, dress, gold, decorum, ceremony and ritual, and being seen and admired now and then, are necessary items with which to balance her personality, as few husbands can understand. Good apparel can thrill her whole being with a fervour that can attain mystical import and make her feel normal.

A woman depends more on what she could be than on what she is. To be a mother or a wife is more binding in its necessity to her than being a father or a husband is to the male concerned. Talkativeness is a vice to which a group of women are more prone than a group of men. Synthetic aspects of intelligence rather than the analytical appeal to women. Details of a practical and necessary life are attended to by her more easily than by men. A good memory, patience, endurance, will and daring too, wherein discretion has full scope, are natural gifts of women.

The man, on the other hand, is distinguished by having more valour than discretion. He belongs to the more overt world of events and actions. Horizontal interests generally hold the centre in the life of the male. The fighting instinct is pronounced in men, and when they fought duels for the sake of some women, the latter enjoyed the fight within themselves as a form of reflected credit to themselves. The warworn soldier or the weather-beaten sailor have charms for the feminine eye, though different from the charms associated with womanhood.

The above indications are by no means exhaustive. They are

yet to be arranged and studied in a methodical manner and in greater detail. That would take us far from the main object of this essay, which is to reveal the verity that, as between the sexes there is implied, not a gradation in degree of development of the psyche as generally thought, but a total polarity as between the two sets of tendencies pertaining to each sex. This principle of polarity, as against mere gradation, is one of the subtle factors in Man-Woman Dialectics which it is very important to recognize.

In order to reveal this polarity in greater relief we have to rely on some of the Greek tragedies that we have already had occasion to cite. The further structure of Man-Woman Dialectics has to be worked out by holding on to common experience on the one hand and to secrets in such tragedies on the other. The great respect in which the tragedies are still held by diverse nations warrants such reliance, and if they did not confer much wisdom, then they should not have deserved, at the hands of modern thinkers, any greater attention or respect than what is given to crime stories in cheap magazines.

A priori and a posteriori, normative and experimental, methods have to be employed by us together, instead of relying on any one exclusively. Some methods could be used to prove both ways, instead of merely unilateral, as in the case when parent and child prove each other, both ways and either way. Womanhood is seen when contrasted with manhood. Manly traits depend on the subtle polarity with those of women for diagnosis, and womanhood would likewise depend on understanding what constitutes manhood. The Absolute is the basis of both variations.

The Terrible Goddess Kālī as the Negative Absolute

In the suicide pacts that lovers sometimes sign, there are two equal and opposite counterparts involved. They are the best of friends and the worst of enemies by virtue of the relation implied. Although the male seems to be outwardly the more active agent, the girl will reveal equally adamantine determination when more closely viewed. Locked in each other's arms, such dead couples in the *Antigone* of Sophocles and in *Hernani* of Hugo reveal the tragedy implicit in Man-Woman Dialectics at its worst. The core of the situation involving reciprocal factors in the context of the neutral Absolute is touched upon and echoed from classical times in the famous lines of Shelley's *Adonais*: "No more let Life divide what Death can join together."

A detailed examination of the masterpiece of Euripides, *Medea*, will reveal between its lines many features of the laws implied. Jason's case belongs totally to the overt horizontal world of values, but in Medea, as the terrible mother who could "steel herself" to such an extent as to gloat over the killing of her own offspring, we have a case of negative absolutism revealed through the soul of womanhood. Poetic justice favours her. She is deified and gains the status of *Kālī* of the Indian context, the feminine personification of Time or Becoming, with its death-dealing potentiality.

Kāla means time and *Kālī* is the feminine aspect of time, which is referred to in the Bhagavad Gita (X.34), as *sarva-hara* (all-devouring). To concede, at least in principle, that every woman represents in her person a spark of the negative principle of the Absolute, which can belch fire when conditions favour its emergence, is the central verity around which Man-Woman Dialectics may be said to turn. If we do not think of life as merely consisting of Herculean tasks but as belonging also equally to a subtler world within, womanhood attains to its position as the core of human affairs.

The Charm of Women

No woman is really beautiful except in the light of the negative absolutism reflected in her personality. No woman can be charming in the same sense as a man can be. An angry Zeus with his thunderbolt has a certain positive charm which the Earth Goddess does not share. In other words, what is recognized as interesting as between the sexes is derived from two distinct and opposing poles. These poles are mutually exclusive yet have a common unitive ground. Spiritually, man and woman have perfect equality or status, but, when they begin to interact, the mode of operation involves the recognition of this polarity as between a positive and a negative Absolute. Such is the secret law regulating Man-Woman Dialectics and it is of the utmost importance for modern man to recognize it in the interest of humanity as a whole. Family relations all over the modernized world tend to be strained because of the absence of this understanding.

A Wise Woman Recognizes Extreme Necessity

The mind can envisage "Contingency" or "Freedom" or the other side of reality which comes under the category "Necessity." A married woman with children to rear cannot afford to minimize the importance of the necessary side of her life, although the man caught in the same context might tend to find a solution lying at the opposite pole of freedom. Escapism comes natural to him; but the more the male talks of freedom in the contingent, the more the female soul stresses the side of extreme necessity.

In the *Medea* of Euripides the Chorus of Women is made to mark the extreme point of necessity which is the regulating factor in women's lives. The possibility of the extinction by death of their offspring is their most natural and deepest concern. After generalizing that most though not all women, in spite of being women, aspire to "culture that dwells in us to teach us wisdom" and that women without children may be left out as having no experience of life, the Chorus is made to say:

> . . . those who have a sweet race of children growing up in their houses do wear away, as I perceive, their whole life through; first with the thought how they may train them up in virtue, next how they shall leave their sons the means to live, and after all this it is far from clear whether on good or bad children they bestow their toil. But one last crowning woe for every mortal I now will name; suppose that they have found sufficient means

> to live and seen their children grow to man's estate and walk in virtue's path, still if fortune so befall, comes Death and bears the children's bodies off to Hades. Can it be any profit to the Gods to heap upon us mortals beside our other woes this further grief for children lost, *a grief surpassing all?*[2]

The italicized tail end of the speech should be noted as intended to mark the extreme limit of the negative absolutist attitude in the care and concern of a mother for her progeny, through which the soul of womanhood is revealed as containing its innermost spark of concern or interest value with all its negative intensity.

The White Heat of Negative Absolutism

When once we have been able to concede that there is something called extreme and absolute negation in the spirit of womanhood, it would be easier to examine its further implications. In this respect the *Medea* of Euripides can be looked upon as a masterly creation, where the soul of womanhood is made to shine, not with the smoky light of negative absolutism as we more often find in its personifications ranging from "Our Lady of Sorrows" onwards through intermediate Madonnas of the various famous master painters, culminating in "La Giaconda" of Leonardo. In the Indian context we have the series ranging from the terrible Kālī, the Dark One, to the bright, white and radiant Sarasvatī sitting on a white lotus. Sophia of Constantinople may be said to come near to this Sanskritized version of the Absolute, seen through the personification of womanhood. In the famous composition of Narayana Guru, *Kālī Ṅāṭakam* — the Dance of Kālī — the positive and negative aspects of the Absolute are brought unitively together as natural to the soul of womanhood. After marking the extreme point of the Absolute Negation, its movement rises gradually to sublime tragic aspects both adorable and terrifying at once.

---

2. *Seven Famous Greek Plays*, Modern Library, New York, p. 327.

Other Implications of the Negative Imperative

That woman is steeped more helplessly in the principle of imperative necessity is well known. When she is past middle age and is burdened with children to look after, the cord that may be said to bind her to the negative pole indicated above is unmistakable. What this kind of bondage implies is to be imagined intuitively in a graded manner as fixing and determining the choice of possible actions in her life which tend to become limited in horizontal possibility, and the bondage is all the more intensely binding to the degree that the femininity represented in her personality is strong.

We have to rely on the writings of those who were correct dialectical critics of human nature, as the Greek Tragic dramatists happened to be, to give actuality of content to statements such as those we have just made, which we confess, necessarily remain very vague in the form we have put them, in the present stage of our formulation of the subject. It is therefore with due apologies that we hearken back more than two thousand years for any known support for our theorization here. The text of Euripides' *Medea* offer us many instances of clarification of this region of Man-Woman Dialectics with which we are at present concerned. We shall therefore use it to examine the import of a few of such instances, taking them in a certain order of importance.

1. THE UNIQUE STATUS OF WOMANHOOD

In passing judgement on womanhood, perhaps one of the errors that males commit, of importance to note, is to judge from norms that apply to manhood. Medea concedes to Jason that, instead of being jealous and rival to the young princess he was going to wed, after putting her and her two sons away, she could have been reasonable enough to see the husband's point of view, and she says strikingly:

> . . . but, I was mad, I who should have shared in these designs, helped on thy plans, and lent my aid to bring about the match, only too pleased to wait upon thy bride. But what we are, we are, we women, evil, I will not say; wherefore thou shouldst not *sink to our sorry level* nor *with our weapons meet our childishness*.[3]

The italicized parts in the above quotation will support the view we have taken of the negative vertical nature of the status of the woman's soul or self. That, though negative and bound by imperative necessity, womanhood is not to be looked upon as an evil but to be met by its own norms and standards, is further emphasized here.

2. NEGATIVE CREATIVENESS OF THE WOMAN'S GENIUS

Schopenhauer and Nietzsche have both discredited women, and in oriental literature it is common to find total depreciation, even going so far as to give support to the belief that women have no soul. This is both true and not at all true if we recognize that Absolutism could find polarized expression both positively and negatively without losing any intrinsic value thereby. Jason, in the quotation below, feels what many reasonable men might feel under similar circumstances.

Explaining how it was in the interests of his children and their mother's comfort at the thought of the second marriage, he concludes his speech of Medea characteristically:

> No, but you women have such strange ideas, that you think all is well so long as your married life runs smooth; but if some mischance occur to ruffle your love, all that was good and lovely erst you reckon as your foes. Yea, men should have begotten children from some other source, no female race existing; thus would evil never have fallen on mankind.[4]

---

3. *Seven Famous Greek Plays*, p. 320.

4. Ibid., p. 301.

Read side by side with the words of Medea earlier, where she refers to the peculiarity of womanhood, the negative absolutism implicit in the soul of womanhood should become sufficiently evident:

> . . . and more than this, we women, though by nature little apt for virtuous deeds, are most expert to fashion any mischief.[5]

This is further confirmed from her earlier words:

> For though women be timorous enough in all else, and as regards courage a coward at the mere sight of steel, yet in the moment she finds her honour wronged, no heart is filled with deadlier thoughts than hers.[6]

3. THE DOUBLE WEIGHT OF NECESSITY FOR WOMEN

The following speech of Medea in regard to the plight of women, speaks for itself most convincingly from a dialectical perspective:

> Of all things that have life and sense, we women are the most hapless creatures; first must be by a husband at great price and over ourselves a tyrant set which is *an evil worse than the first;* and herein lies the most important issue, whether our choice is good or bad. For divorce is not honourable to women, nor can we disown our lords. Next, must the wife coming as she does to ways and customs new since she has not learnt the lesson in her home, have a *diviner eye* to see how best to treat the partner of her life. If haply we perform these tasks with thoroughness and tact, and the husbands live with us, without resenting the yoke, our life is a happy one; if not *it were best to die.* But when a man is vexed with what he finds indoors he goes forth and rids his soul of its disgust, betaking him to some friend or comrade of like age; whilst we (women) must needs regard his single self.[7]

The implication of the italicized words in the above quotation,

5. *Seven Famous Greek Plays*, p. 304.
6. Ibid., p. 299.
7. Ibid., p. 298.

when examined closely, will bring out how a frustrated marriage is more than a mere failure, but implies a double disaster. There is a gambler's gain or loss rather than loss or gain in a merely business sense.

4. WOMAN IS OUT OF HER ELEMENT IN THE HORIZONTAL

When Medea admits to Jason, saying "woman is a weak creature ever given to tears,"[8] and again says that her rival princess whom Jason wishes to marry could be won over by the glamour of shining presents which she describes as the "garniture of death," and adds that, being a woman like her, she could persuade her to be kind to her children, the limits of the world of vertical values within whose range the spirit of womanhood naturally lives and moves are clearly demarcated for us by Euripides. This verity is further clarified by the following words between Medea and Jason:

Medea :	May that prosperity whose end is woe never be mine and such wealth as would ever sting my heart.
Jason :	Change that prayer as I will teach thee, and thou wilt show more wisdom. Never let happiness appear in sorrow's guise nor when thy fortune smiles pretend she frowns.[9]

Medea here thinks in terms of a long-span interest in time, while the wisdom recommended by the male has a shorter span of life-interest in respect of the same family, with which both are equally concerned.

Possessiveness and Killing Kindness

Because of her own position in the negative vertical aspect of the Absolute Consciousness, a woman exercises strong influences on her male counterpart which mere rationalism might brush aside

8. *Seven Famous Greek Plays*, p. 321.

9. Ibid., p. 309.

lightly as a factor of negligible importance. When we know that even a pet animal can bind a person for a lifetime to a locality or pattern of behaviour, it would be unwise dialectically to say that relationship with a woman, when some bipolarity has developed, is one that can be lightly overcome. As gravity pulls objects to the centre of the earth, there is a negative lag in man's relation with women, which is a factor to be accounted very real in the relational set-up into which all men find themselves fitted. The first effect of the negative pull is to stifle all initiative and action in the male. He begins to resign himself when overpowered and, in certain cases, even with strong men the defeat can be so complete that it amounts to a moribund state of the spirit.

There are two Greek plays in which this feature of the dialectics of womanhood is brought in very strikingly. When reference is made (in Sophocles' *The Women of Trachis*) by Deianeira the wife of Herakles, to a tunic which was meant to be

> a present for my husband
> Of my own making.

which, according to her instructions,

> no one but he must put it on or touch it;
> Nor must it be exposed to the light of the sun.

It is meant to honour him and mark the end of his labours. For taking the tunic and delivering it to Herakles, who is still to arrive home, Deianeria significantly adds that, for the kindness of the messengers towards both herself and Herakles, "*both* will thank you." When we remember that this magic shirt is given with the best of intentions by a wife who has overcome her jealousy and only honours his homecoming, the absolute nature of the negativity implicit in her kindness is underlined by Sophocles. The effect that the tunic of the most loving and devoted of wives still has, according to the author, is described in Herakles' own words as follows:

> This is the worst of all the famous burdens
> This body has shouldered, all the hot encounters
> These hands have fought in, none was ever like it
> The wife of Zeus — the tyrannous Eurystheus —
> None of them laid such heavy pains upon me
> As that false-smiling woman, Oineus' daughter
> Who wrapped me in this garment of damnation,
> This net to strangle me. Stuck fast upon me
> It has devoured my vitals inch by inch,
> Sucked out the channels of my breath, and drunk
> My living blood — a man without a body
> Imprisoned in a death that has no name!
> No warrior's spear, no army of earth-born giants,
> No savage beast, no Greek, no alien tongue,
> No land of all I have fought to cleanse,
> Did such a thing to me. One woman,
> Unmanly woman, unarmed, has vanquished me.[10]

Although put in figurative pictorial language, the negative principle of killing kindness and the backward pull of possessiveness in the best of women dialectically related with man, becomes quite evident here. It could only be the principle of negative absolutism in women that could counter the labours of a divinity like Herakles and bring them to such a close.

Man-Woman Dialectics More Unitively Conceived

The rival goddesses Aphrodite and Artemis represent two types of women as different as Martha and Mary of the Bible (*Luke*, X.38-42) or like Kātyāyanī and Maitreyī of the Upanishads. Women who are themselves dialectical counterparts to one another can live as co-admirers, disciples or even as wives of the same central figure represented by the man who teaches the neutral Absolute and represents it in his own person. Thus Yājñavalkya the ancient *ṛṣi* (sage) of the Upanishads is said to have had two wives, who are described and contrasted in the following words:

10. *Electra and Other Plays*, Penguin, p. 153.

> Now then, Yājñavalkya had two wives, Maitreyī and Kātyāyanī. Of the two, Maitreyī was a discourser on the Wisdom of the Absolute (*brahma-vidyā*). Kātyāyanī had just (*eva*) a woman's understanding of such a subject.
>
> — *Bṛhadāraṇyaka Upanishad*, IV.v.1

When the sage was about to leave them both, after giving all his properties to them, the Artemis type of wife, the younger Maitreyī, asks: "What should I do with that wealth through which I may not be immortal? What you *know*, sir, that indeed tell me." The Upanishad continues:

> Then Yājñavalkya said: "Ah, my dear! dear as you are to us, more dear is what you say! Come, sit down. I will explain to you. But while I am explaining, do you seek to ponder thereon." Then he said: "Lo, verily, not for love of the husband is the husband dear, but for the love of the Self (*Ātman*) a husband is dear."

Then there follows a series of similar values, "wife," "sons," "cattle," "brāhmaṇahood," "kṣātrahood," "worlds," "gods," "Vedas," "beings," culminating in the generalization,

> Lo, verily, not for the love of all is all dear, but for the love of the Self is all dear. — Ibid., IV.v.6[11]

The Self here would stand for the unitive Absolute, and the teacher of the Absolute, in representing the neutrality of the Absolute, is neither husband nor wife but belongs to the context of pure wisdom which gives no room for relativistic jealousies or rivalries. This episode proves the possibility of both men and women conforming to unitive dialectics in the context of the Absolute.

11. The reader may see R.E. Hume's *The Thirteen Principal Upanishads* which has a reliable translation. There are two places in the *Bṛhadāraṇyaka* (Great Forest) *Upanishad* where the same episode, (II.iv, and IV.v) appears, pp. 98 and 144 of Hume.

Devotion Between Husband and Wife

Even outside the context of pure wisdom which we have considered just now, the relation between husband and wife viewed from the contemplative dialectical angle presents quite another picture to that taken by moderns. Narayana Guru puts the case trenchantly in his *Darśana-Mālā* (Garland of Visions) as follows.

> Wife adores the husband
> (As) the husband the wife
> Not for nothing (at all):
> Self-Bliss verily do they adore
> Implicitly present in all sense pleasures.
>
> He who can thus see everywhere,
> For him, the wise one, besides Self-Bliss
> There remains nothing at all!
> Such adoration is greater indeed than all!
> — *Darśana-Mālā,* VIII.7-8

Instead of sense-pleasure being looked upon as part of the original sin of man, we find it here exalted to the status of an important aspect of Self-Bliss which belongs to the contemplation of the Absolute. The age-long slur on sex pleasure is here abolished and a revised and revalued status is given even to conjugal life in the context of full-fledged wisdom. When conjugal happiness will again be conceived in the light of such a thoroughgoing wisdom, the stigma on married life and some of the contempt for women as something to be shunned in the name of spiritual life, will tend to disappear. Women would gain a revised status as equal partners in man's life, even of the most contemplative order.

Promiscuity vs. Dialectical Sex Relations

In the normal family, in an ordered society and co-educational institutions it is important to think in terms of the Man-Woman Dialectics that we have developed in order that much absurdity, nuisance and ugliness may be avoided. Subtle eugenics, not to speak of healthy psycho-physical development, is likely to be tampered with when promiscuity prevails. What nature teaches on one side, modified suitably by the wisdom that takes both the sexes together into consideration, rather than unilaterally, should be brought to bear on the problem of the intercourse, cooperation, or common educational enterprise that men and women may undertake as dialectical counterparts.

Both austere separation and promiscuous intercourse would be undesirable. The most central of facts that we have tried to lay bare, which consists of recognizing the polarity, as between the sexes, must always be kept in mind, and the relations in various contexts so regulated that the best both in manhood and womanhood can get a chance of affirmation in the personality of either sex, instead of being both suppressed and atrophied by lack of chance to shine in each other's eyes. The law of double loss and double gain is again involved here. We shall examine how this is so in the three contexts of co-education, mixed co-operative colonies or *āśrama*s, and in the family unit itself.

Applied Dialectics in Co-Educational Institutions

Modern trends in co-educational institutions have gone far in the direction of making sex without meaning, flavour or taste. Sex, as exercised whether among animals or humans, has always an alternating element of hide and seek. The girl recedes while the boy asserts himself. The mirror which reflects the charms of an adolescent girl tells her more vital stories about herself than to her male counterpart who is more keen on looking than on being looked at. Boys who are "sissies" and "tomboy" girls have better chances of rubbing off their angularities that are monstrosities and out of place in either of them, by a healthy commingling of boys and girls. Admiring mutually, they tend to become better and better. The boy would like to shine in the eyes of the girl who is his favourite and vice versa. When the dialectical balance and orientation is upset or inversely conceived, double degeneracy would set in, tending to make sex insipid and even absurd for a lifetime.

The Guru Narayana once remarked that co-education would be beneficial if the boys could admire the girls and the girls the boys, so that both parties could improve thereby. A positive orientation has however to be steadily maintained so that a better synthesis evolves out of the thesis and antithesis implicit in the situation as between the sexes. To work out details of the *modus operandi* would take us beyond the scope of the present essay.

In Co-operative Communities or Āśramas

In co-operative or other community organizations where men and women live, wisdom would require in the first instance that there be at least two main departments, one where the interests of one sex are looked after, and the other for the protection and safeguarding of values peculiar to the other sex. If a couple happen to be at the helm of affairs, it would always be safe to divide the functions, so that general confusion in the world of relationships as within the members, male or female, of the community may not become more confounded.

Like wrong connections of wires in a delicate electrical machine the whole situation may become over-heated and blown up if the plus and minus of the situation are ignored. The poles represented by the sexes must each gather round them the loyalty and obedience of the person immediately at the head of each pole, and if further integration is to be attempted, it should only be in the name of a neutral, absolutist or presiding value in the person of a wise, generous, and non-interfering head who would be a witness and critic merely of the various active aspects of the institution. The guiding principles derived from the Absolute would be what he would neutrally represent in his person, without active interference.

It would be a further good rule also to remember that the relations as between one member and another, or one disciple and another of each of the two sections, should be of a minimum, and the bipolar relation between the heads of the two main sections and their respective wards or dependents should be as direct, bipolar and as maximal as possible to either party involved. As we avoid short-circuiting in electrical wiring, these dialectical considerations derived from the polarity of the sexes and the two aspects of the Absolute that they can represent, is a matter of utmost importance. Any neglect of detail or absence of proper insulation might blow up the whole apparatus.

Man-Woman Dialectics in the Family Unit

Couples, when they are happy, are doubly so, and with the slightest tilting of the dialectical balance of the scales they can become more miserable than if they did not live at all. This, however, should not be understood as a recommendation to commit double suicide, but only to enable them to guide their lives intelligently so as to bring enhanced happiness to both. Husband and wife should keep apart and come together only if double benefit is derivable from both separation and union. The further elaboration of this subject would again take us beyond the scope of this essay.

The Crossing Swords of Outer Duels and Inner Gossip

In the Middle Ages duels were fought over women in which one or both who drew the swords could have died. This happens in the overt world of events where a beautiful girl may happen to live. In the corresponding innate world of rumour, gossip also draws daggers in regard to her virtue among the women themselves who might talk about the love affair at the village well. If steel swords can kill men, gossip can kill the good repute of women with equal fatality.

In Goethe's *Faust* Gretchen was a simple village girl whose absolute womanhood was a value which was exposed to both these factors of murder with swords and words at once. They killed her both morally and spiritually and drove her mad.

In *The Women of Trachis* of Sophocles we have the case of Iole, the silent but beautiful princess for whom for prize Herakles in the last of his labours sacked her father's city and sent her as prisoner to his own home. His legitimate wife Deianeira is wise enough with extreme discretion to overcome her rivalry to this young and "silent beauty" from whom, as she sees them among the captive women, she could get no word of response to her kind inquiries. Iole is further referred to as the "nameless woman" by one of the messengers and again as a "great name and a great beauty." Deianeira herself is able to pity her and forgive her husband's partiality for her and says characteristically, referring to the various loves of her husband:

> I never blamed and scolded any of them
> Nor this one though she be melted heart and soul
> In the fire of her love; because I am sorry for her;
> Because her beauty has been her ruin, and she
> Unwittingly has brought her country down
> To slavery and destruction.[12]

On her side, Deianeira herself generalizes elsewhere as follows:

> Can any woman lose the precious name
> Of virtue in which she trusted, and still live
> Branded with shame?[13]

Virtue and good repute are well known to be of vital importance to the soul of womanhood. A sense of shame with which womanhood is endowed more than man (who might have honour for its overt counterpart) can prove a life or death value for many noble women. Only *absolute virtue* in a beautiful woman can save

---

12. *Electra and Other Plays*, Penguin, p. 135.
13. Ibid., p. 143.

her soul from becoming the storm centre of catastrophes great or small, that can have her as their common locus. Iole, the silent, young and beautiful princess in *The Women of Trachis,* is evidently meant to be an absolutist woman of the sad and silent type. This is amply confirmed by the reference to her as the match of the demi-god Herakles himself in words such as the following:

> Great are the victories of Herakles —
> But here, in love, he met his match.

If we remember that the titans and Herakles himself are meant to represent the Dionysiac principle of the Absolute as known to Greek tragedy and ritual, the lines quoted above to the effect that a silent and almost unnamed beauty could be his match, then we can come to recognize in the soul of womanhood the ultimate terms of negative absolutism.

Caught between masculine prowess or honour and feminine virtue or reputation for chastity, womanhood represents a personal value in human life which calls for the greatest precautions of wisdom to deal with. Men and women have to live and love in the vague world of rumour, and when horizontal factors are introduced, whether in the form of haughty self-assertion of the male, or mere gossip, a very volatile or inflammable situation can develop unawares, requiring the highest discretion on the part of all concerned.

It is not the intelligent woman that the world needs, but rather more and more women of good reputation. Womanhood represents Creative Becoming in Nature and the vital urge implicit in the soul of woman can look silent and weak, but its potential possibilities surpass any other factor. In the *Kālī Nāṭaka* (Dance of Kālī) composed by the Guru Narayana we have this negative absolutism personified in all its dark yet splendid glory.

6

The Sacredness of Sex

PRUDERY is a byproduct of civilization. Cavemen cannot be imagined as subject to this subtle vice. They were protected by a natural honesty. Later on, in the progressive development of human life through different phases, sex became taboo. The sacred became contrasted with the profane, in the name of unseen values. Doctrines of original sin and man's fall from his birthright of purity, and salvation through grace or merit began to influence the human conscience. Sex and sin have been considered almost synonymous in the religious context of Buddhism no less than Christianity — two of the world's greatest religious growths. The happy state of natural innocence was overcovered by guilt-sense obsessions and repressions from which humanity has continued to suffer, and from which, to a large extent, humanity still suffers.

When sex became a matter of shame rather than one of pride as with ancient peoples, marriage became discredited in favour of celibacy. Women became despised. A married saint was an exception. Heloise became dishonourable to the spirituality of Abelard and the rumoured love of Joan of Arc was enough to kill her spiritual reputation. Rousseau's name became anathema to the orthodox. Much sex hypocrisy, however, passed unnoticed under the cloak of monasticism.

To consider sex as necessary or normal smacks of paganism or heresy even today. It was only recently that Freudian psychology entered by the back door of academic life and created a stir. Notions about sex and sin are being revised drastically by the modern generation. It is time to rethink of this matter with thoroughness.

The Absolute as Eros

Vedic texts are not religious in the same sense that Christianity follows, because their "paganism" is sometimes shockingly sexy. Even when the Vedas give place to the Upanishads which hold up the models of wisdom and renunciation, this Vedic attitude to sex has persisted. Max Müller preferred to translate some too honest Upanishadic passages into Latin rather than plain English, like the other parts of the text, in the name of decency. The Bhagavad Gita which continues and upholds the Vedic tradition and way of life in a revalued form goes even as far as to state that the Absolute itself consists of *Kāma*, the erotic value-factor, when not against righteous conduct (VII. 11). Cupidity and concupiscence are not such sins as the active objective aspects of desire or anger such as implied in *rajas*, the active pursuit of desire. (The subtle difference between the two forms of desire or attachment is clearly implied in the Gita, III.7.)

The four ends of human life (*puruṣārtha*s), viz., righteousness (*dharma*), wealth (*artha*), value-motive (*kāma*) and release (*mokṣa*) glaringly include this urge for full living called *kāma* as an important component of a purposeful life. The Upanishads refer to spiritual betterment (*śreyas*) and here and now values in life (*preyas*) as both desirable even to a spiritual aspirant.

Erotic Mysticism

When we touch the stratum prior to the Vedas, sex looms large in it. We have referred to the sacredness of fecundity and virility of prehistoric man. The worship of the phallus (*liṅgam*) is an unmistakable indication. This tendency has culminated in the androgynous god Śiva who is an unrepressed Bacchus in whom sex attains to a high sanctity. In him male and female meet in a Sex which is with a capital S.

Some ancient South Indian temples have images of divinities to whom nudism is normal, and representations of coitus in frieze or panel are so common that passers-by take them for granted, while even a modern tourist boasting of "free morals" might well be shocked out of his wits by them. The subtle dialectical interplay between the profane and the sacred as preserved in such ancient places of worship is at least the joy of the dilettante at present.

In and through the bane and taboo of sex, however, it persists and flourishes in the very precincts of religion. Erotic mysticism has its place at the core of the sacred scriptures themselves. The *Song of Songs* of the Bible and *Gīta Govinda* (aptly translated *Indian Song of Songs* by Sir Edwin Arnold) are glaring examples of this ironical phenomenon. The Pastoral Kṛṣṇa's morality with the cowherd girls cannot be easily explained away by Hindu apologists who wish to see their favourite deity appear more respectable in the eyes of other critics. This is because they are beginning to forget the idiom or language proper to contemplative mysticism. Sanskrit, though "dead" as a modern tongue, lives by virtue of contemplative values it preserves. Sex and love find in it a natural habitat. This "civilized language of the gods" (*devabhāṣā*) combines sex and love delectably into a pure joy legitimate to man. Vulgarity becomes impossible here because of its primitive purity.

Due Place for Sex

Whether sex made men feel morally or spiritually inferior or superior, it has been present all through and has exerted its pressure in human life almost uniformly from the beginning. Talk of controlling it or suppressing it is out of the question. (The Gita recognizes this verity of the irrepressible nature of vital tendencies in III.33: "Even a man of wisdom behaves in conformity with his own nature. All creation goes on subject to nature. Of what avail is control?") Human decency makes us ashamed of it and we vainly try to abolish it, but the more intelligent way would be to give it its due place in human life and to take full advantage of its potentialities to raise the level of human goodness or perfection.

Rousseau in Europe first broke the stigma of sex taboo by composing simple love songs. Then came psychologists and educators who advocated co-education and a free development of the personality. Bergson's epoch-making work touched the core of the problem in *The Two Sources of Morality and Religion*, as the title itself indicates. He established here that there is a mystical morality which is free, dynamic and open, as opposed to a social morality which is closed, static and obligatory in character. These stages in the development of modern thought have made the modern adolescent thinker very alive to the problem of sex.

Art and Contemplation

Spurious or sensational literature on this subject, whether in the name of *brahmacarya* (a much misunderstood term), or, on the other side, "psychiatry" or "psychopathology" which is swallowed down with avidity by modern readers, is helping to confound and confuse adolescents. Maladjusted and distorted personalities arise out of a perverted attitude to this item of life urge.

The faint line which divides lewdness from a liberally educated refinement or good taste, especially in the field of art, is an elusive one. Good taste actually involves an element of wisdom, which latter depends on equalizing two opposing tendencies within human nature. It is art that can help in sublimating sex and making it pure. The principle of sacrifice (*yajña*) referred to in the Gita[1] which the Creator put into human beings at the very start of creation, is the other potent factor which can lift mere sex and transform its value contemplatively into something noble and

1. III.10: "In ancient times, having created the peoples with sacrifice as pertaining to them (necessary), Prajāpati (the Lord of the Peoples) said 'By this shall you grow and multiply. Let this be to you the milchcow of all desires.'"

sublime. Sex has to be canalized and made to flow through contemplative channels.

The Epic of Kālidāsa

A supreme example of a whole epic composition devoted to this subject is found in *The Birth of the War God* (*Kumāra-sambhava*) of Kālidāsa. Shakespeare or Dante could also be quoted with equal advantage.

Here we return again to the story of the ancient people's god Śiva, whom stone-language and myth conceived as androgynous. Here in this epic, one of the twin aspects of the Absolute as represented by the Daughter of Himalaya (Pārvatī), representing nature, meets Śiva the Supreme Man (*Puruṣa*). Resulting from their union is the positive spiritual principle Subrahmaṇya or Kumāra who is also known as the "War God" in Sanskrit as the vanquisher of all dark forces or forces of relativism. He represents the victory of the Absolute.

The striking feature of this epic that we should notice here is that Śiva burnt to ashes Eros the God of Love. This sharp tragic note is at the core of the epic. Sex or love of a different order, however, pervades the whole epic and every metaphor or figure of speech reveals a philosophical scheme of reality into which sacred love enters to reveal the good, the true or the beautiful in life. Sex in its most intimate aspects is not excluded from the string of graded interests which the master-poet fingers alternatingly. The dialectical paradox round which the epic is constructed consists of the fact that while the flame emitted by the middle eye of Śiva tragically reduces Kāma (Eros) to ashes as Rati (the consort of Eros) watches on weeping and voices of unseen spectators call for mercy through the winds, Śiva himself is not without his love affair with Pārvatī. This develops at the pace of eternal becoming. Pārvatī undergoes long penances for the favour of Śiva in the forest where he meditates.

Sheer Joy

After long austerities, standing in neck-deep water or in scorching sun or in rain, emaciated, with pallor invading all but the redness of her lips, Pārvatī makes an offering to Śiva in meditation in mid-forest. The eyes of Śiva open in sympathy that has nothing but sacred love implicit in it, but when the eyes light inadvertently on the red lips of Pārvatī, Kāma (Eros) is about to assert himself readily aiming an arrow at Śiva at that moment of rare advantage.

The God meets the situation by the burning of Kāma with all tragic vehemence or indignation. This inner happening, depicted in overt epic form, gives us the secret of this noble poem, in which Love or Sex with a capital letter that knows no decrease, is contrasted with sex that passes and fades like summer's blossoms. Relativist and Absolutist values with sex and love as its central items are here juxtaposed, compared and contrasted masterfully. Sex attains a sacred status here. Art, philosophy, morals and mysticism come together to accomplish this task. The subtle dialectical interplay of sex and love values can be seen in this composition to weave the fabric of a sheer joy which is sublime and sacred at once, in spite of sex or love being the central interest.

7

The Enigma of the Smile of Mona Lisa

When men and women who claim to be cultured meet in Europe, conversation soon turns round the familiar subject of art criticism. Hardly had I landed in Europe this time when I found myself assailed many times in after-dinner conversations by questions such as whether I liked modern or classical art. Impressionism, surrealism, cubism, the *clair-obscur* of Rembrandt and the famous painting of the sacrifice of the Holy Lamb by Van Eyke were natural topics raised. Some went into details of technique in the matter of line, light or colour. Many talked about the proportions and the secret geometry kept in mind by the artist which followed the principle of the "golden number" supposed to be derived from Plato but christened as such, centuries later, by Leonardo da Vinci.

"The Last Supper" by da Vinci, the original of which I had looked at in Milan, nearly thirty years ago now, has remained in my memory together with what I have seen in the most famous galleries of Venice, Vicenza, Naples, Rome, Padua and in the Sistine Chapel of the Vatican. I have heard many guides and read many stray articles and books about art. I must confess, however, that the key to the true appreciation of art still eludes me. It seems now that I have to be taught from the very beginning.

Breakdown of Art Criticism

Did art critics still think in terms of definitions? Some did, but this was very rare. Others, including some that I met who had taken a five-year course of the history of European art, cared for no norms or definitions at all. They were often carried away by merely superficial techniques. Even here, if, for instance, one asked what was the greatness of a Picasso, Van Gogh, Goya, or a Cezanne, one was only answered vaguely with exclamations, shruggings of shoulders, superlatives, ravishments, or other forms of linguistic exaggerations such as "I adore" or "I hate." Europe that takes pride in what Romain Rolland called the *Libre Critique d'Occident* flounders at present totally when it comes to clear notions on art.

I am selecting here one item which has always intrigued me, namely, the place that we have to give to Leonardo da Vinci's *La Giaconda*, better known as Mona Lisa, in the whole range of masterpieces of European art that comes naturally within the purview of any art critic who wishes to be systematic. In my view this major problem is inseparably linked with the eternal enigma of the oblique smile of Mona Lisa.

The Obsession with La Giaconda

The sensation that prevailed in the world of art when this famous painting hanging in a very cherished and important place in the museum of the Louvre in Paris, was stolen not so long ago, indicates that it still occupies a central position as a supreme example of Western art taken as a whole. Even now the sensation round this painting has not subsided.

Although there are many now in Europe who pooh-pooh the idea of giving this painting any central place in discussions, the subject is one that haunts the subconscious of the art critic in a strange manner. I recently had a lively discussion on this subject with a middle-aged lady, who had herself recently turned from being a talented portrait painter to a sort of impressionism that relied on vague and nebulous patchy colour-patterns without any figures as such. My attention was drawn to other painters who were to be treated as more important than Leonardo, even for historical reasons. After this I felt quite discouraged about being able to hold my own in any conversation on the subject of art. To my surprise I found that the universities no more began by the definition of art. Art criticism had become a matter of merely individual taste. Plato and Aristotle were long outmoded here. One like me, who desired to see all branches of culture hang together by a central notion, had to suffer some disillusionment and discouragement.

However, I happened to pick up a popular illustrated magazine, called the *Paris Match* of 13 June 1959 and found to my surprise that therein was reproduced a modern version of the Mona Lisa, holding some gold dollars in her palm and caricatured with a pointed Kaiser moustache on the otherwise same face, except that the eyes were fully open and the enigmatic smile was slightly changed into one that was harsher. Extracts from the note below the picture read as follows when translated:

> The smile of Mona Lisa has always tormented painters, impenetrable secret before which all the resources of their talents were spent away. Salvador Dali has made his own portrait "after the manner of" in order to free himself in turn from this obsession.

Modern painters evidently hardly know what to make out of this painting any more. The dollars that have been put there by Salvador Dali and the name given to his work *Avida Dollars* represent the tendency of modern painters to laugh altogether at this masterpiece. It survives as something hardly more than a joke at the present day.

Leonardo and Bergson

Now let us turn to the words of a philosopher of scarcely a generation ago, Henri Bergson, who wrote or rather spoke on the subject of this very Mona Lisa of Leonardo. Quoting first from Leonardo da Vinci's *Traite de Peinture* directly, we read:

> The secret of the art of drawing is to discover in each object the particular manner in which there is along the whole of its extension a certain direction such as that of the central wave which expresses itself in the form of superficial waves, a certain undulating line which is, as it were, its generating axis.

Commenting further himself on the secret that Leonardo explains above, Bergson, apropos Mona Lisa, continues as follows:

> True art seeks to render the individuality of a model and for this goes to seek behind the lines that one sees, the movement which the eye does not see, behind the very movement itself, something that is more secret, the original intention, the fundamental aspiration of the person, a simple thought which would be equal to the undefined richness of forms and colours.[1]

On the single subject of Mona Lisa we thus find opinions that are very sharply divided. Some like Bergson see in it what the ordinary man can hardly see without initiation, and some others laugh at it altogether. It is the latter tendency that I see gaining ground now, new standards of art quickly replacing the old. One would even feel that the age of classical art from Raphael and Michelangelo through religious art like the Pieta of Avignon, Van Eyke and Rubens, to its latest representatives in Minne (the father of my hostess), is coming to a close. The art of Edgar Gevaert is an example of how modern art is striking a new line in which Christian and pagan art counterbalance each other. "To have something better to do than paint Mona Lisa" has even become a current idiom among certain sections of painters, as has been reported in the very article of *Paris Match* quoted above.

The smile of Mona Lisa has thus become a sort of sore spot, a touchy subject or what might be called a complex to the dilettante and the serious or light-hearted art critic of the present day. Even directors of studies about the history of art seem no more able to

1. *La Pensee et le Mouvant*, Bergson, Geneva, p. 248.

say anything intelligible about it. Meanwhile, even by wilful omission, it becomes more and more an obsession.

What we have to offer ourselves to the discussion will be conceived from the dialectical angle and would be based on the philosophy of the distinction between the self and the non-self.

8

How Yoga Solves Social Problems

THE seasons come and go while man sits contemplating them. They are both inside and outside at once. A constant fire burns within while the winds blow, the rain falls, the good earth sustains with its solidity and rivers spread their waters around. Where the inner events end and the outer start is hard to determine definitely while we witness the subtle interplay of forces as they ebb or flow or burn brightly or dimly with each breath we take or let out. Such is the neutral psycho-physical magic of the colourful world of waking that alternates with the dull grey, black or white of inner life.

To see all with unitive equanimity in the sameness of the whole is the core of the contemplative way. After much study and travel, laborious research and easy days of relaxation, I find myself, as my days ripen and mature, sitting in cross-legged meditation in the cool atmosphere of the hills, more and more composed within myself. The sunshine and breezes still influence me with their changing moods that are within me and reflected in outward conditions. Many an August and September day thus went by, meeting its counterpart at dawn or dusk in my solitary reveries. I changed with the patterns that wove their thin fabrics around me, and sat still too within the privacy of my own inner life. I have at last been trying to meditate and begun seriously to taste some of its delights. Such is the event which is really no event, which formed the content of my consciousness these recent days.

The brighter days of the end of August and the beginning of September were mostly uneventful otherwise.

Insularity and Openness

Peninsular India with its insularity and the open breezes that sweep over the seas of the Indian archipelago are also twin aspects that coexist geographically, while seasons come and go inducing their colourful or duller moods in man. The whole, globally sensed and understood, constitutes the joy of contemplative life. Man is at peace when the whole is contemplated continuously, but conflicts come and banish his peace of mind when dual forces are allowed to alternate according to a natural rhythm for man to a life worth living. Otherwise it becomes all labour and turmoil. Insulation and openness meet in the unitive globality of thought and feeling in the Absolute to be known and felt at once.

Thus harmonized perfectly now and imperfectly at another moment, life, inner and outer, takes its alternating course, while the self sits within witnessing its own peripheral phenomenological chain of events glowing or growing dim or burning with a brightness that knows no bounds. What is at the core is hardly experienced and is beyond words, while the passing show of peripheral consciousness streams out of its basic nothingness.

Laziness and Hard Labour

Hard labour is a recognized form of punishment; so also is laziness which makes a devil's workshop in the mind.

There have been endless polemics on the rival claims of these subjects by religious, philosophical or sociological theorists. Piety and works have been opposed in the West, as *karma* (action) and *jñāna* (wisdom) have also been the subjects of endless philosophical discussions in the history of philosophical thought in India.

In these days of five-year plans and pragmatic values, work is placed on a pedestal and worshipped in the name of increased production, of what is vaguely termed progress. The pastoral civilization of the Todas contrasts with the rush and haste which the New York Fifth Avenue and Empire State Building seem to glorify. Modernism looks askance at contemplation as a sheer waste of time. Our sense of values has to be re-established on some new scientific basis before we can cultivate the more deep-seated aspects of our personality.

The West is beginning to recognize this depth aspect while the East, which is famed for its wisdom, is losing its hold on just this aspect of life which educated men in the West are beginning to recognize more and more. Youth in the Orient is turning its eyes to Western standards of outer values. This constitutes the tragedy of modernism which deserves to be better understood.

Impact of Modernism on Pastoral People

Our thoughts have lingered, in recent days, all the more on the Todas, the pastoral people of an ideal Rousseau Utopia, who have, as we have seen, their own valid notions of civilization and progress. With a Toda lady who has been subjected to the process of civilization and modernization, both by religious and governmental agencies, I have had several tête-à-têtes recently in the company of some others interested in the Todas.

The Todas are rapidly getting civilized in the wrong sense. Drink has taken the vacancy once filled by natural pastoral leisureliness. Their self-sufficient and simple economy has been disrupted by conscious or unconscious interference. Their problems have increased instead of decreasing. They do not know which way to turn for solace and are at present like many other natural remnants of the past preserved discontinuously in protected parts or reserves the world over, who are becoming more and more an anachronism and eyesore.

The Secret of Re-integration of Lost Peoples

Tribals, primitive people, undeveloped or underdeveloped countries, backward parts of the world, are various nicknames applied to peoples maladjusted to what passes for progress or civilization.

Work and virtue seem to be considered synonymous to the modernist. Work, work and more work seems to be the accepted slogan in certain quarters, while on the other side the stress hitherto has been on the restfulness of the Sabbath day. The relation between the Sabbath and weekdays has to be understood in a dialectically revised way, if the accentuation of the one at the expense of the other, both tending to an unhealthy imbalance in life, is to be avoided.

Herein is a secret. Piety and works, knowledge and action, Vedism and Vedāntism, can be put together vertically without conflict, but when horizontal elements enter into them, they become vitiated by a dualism that would spoil the case of both. The almost good can never be good enough, as almost winning a prize, or almost jumping across a gap can be worse than nothing at all. Lukewarm belief in God might be worse than downright atheism. A correct sceptic can be a better believer than one who believes wrongly in a secondary god. In bringing civilization or light, these subtle considerations have to be given their place as mechanistic solutions can be worse than anything at all.

A Science of Normal Human Values

Sitting over a cup of tea one August evening with a Toda lady and three others, I tried to expound by way of table talk some of my ideas about helping the Todas, instead of interfering with them as most often people do in the name of God, Crown or Country.

The effects of such tampering with the ways of life of a free self-satisfied and peace-loving people had so far failed. There was something fundamentally wrong. In what respects was the attitude to be revised? This seemed a simple question, but to answer it in a simple straightforward, commonsense way was not easy at all. The whole matter consists in understanding the difference between what makes for horizontal interference and in merely allowing a vertical influence to operate in and through and for the group concerned, as if from inside rather than as from patronizing or proselytizing outsiders.

The difference is fundamental and vital but nonetheless subtle. Doles of generosity will only degenerate the receivers further. Concessions might cut against the general grain of social structure and do much damage in principle for little practical good gained. Favouritism might make them sink lower into dependent servility. The common arguments are that the forces of modernism are sure to operate on these selected peoples too for whatever they are worth, good or bad; such is the force of compelling circumstances, that economic forces have to enter every corner, and standards have to rise uniformly or not at all; that retrospective revivalism has to be avoided since man cannot begin to walk on all fours like animals, although they might have evolved originally from a common animal ancestor. These are some of the ready arguments that one hears so often.

Soon the question loses all chances of a hearing at all, and all is given up as hopeless. Superficialities overcover the whole problem and all ends in smoke.

The Mechanistic and the Dialectical Approaches

A different way of approaching the problem is possible. One can look through a telescope at the wrong end. A blinded man examining a jar held upside down could make the double error of finding no opening at the top and a hole at the bottom, making it doubly useless, which could be rectified when the jar is examined correctly beheld with open eyes.

Such errors are characteristically dialectical and not merely logical. Surd and absurd, sense and nonsense, light and darkness, are often related by a double-sided dialectical relationship. Many jokes are based on the same kind of error of judgement.

There are many questions in which the mechanistic approach just makes no sense while the dialectical one gives fruitful indications. The problem of Arjuna (Bhagavad Gita II. 5-6)[1] as stated by himself (rather than by others uninitiated into the dialectical way) is one that typifies the common error of seeing mechanistic answers to problems that are to be solved through dialectics alone. As in the joke of a husband who was asked by his wife, when it was raining, to see to the leak in the roof, excusing himself for a good reason when it was still wet weather, and just neglecting the work when it was clear weather, saying the need was not pressing, some reasons are not only one-legged, but might fall, like the rider, on the other side of the horse, by overleaping the mark.

Paradoxes can be solved by a middle path which lives between logical contradictions and mere tautologies. A vertical axis of right higher reasoning runs through these two poles marked by these limits set by horizontal mechanistic logic. This higher logic, which has been called dialectic by Plato and recognized as *yoga* in Indian thought, is a rare human heritage that tends to be lost over and over again in human history. Modernism in the hands of a Wells, a Julian Huxley or a Peirce, often reveals a lack of the depth aspect of higher wisdom.

---

1. "Desisting from the killing of gurus who are highly honourable, it would be more meritorious in this world even to have to eat of a beggar's pittance. Choosing (on the other hand) to kill these gurus as fortune-seekers, I should be feasting even here on blood-stained benefits of life. Neither is it clear which would be of greater advantage to me; that we win or that they win over us. Killing whom we should no more wish to live, those very persons are standing ranged before us, the progeny of Dhṛtarāṣṭra."

It might be true that as a reaction against the extreme hair-splitting and logic-chopping of scholastic theologians this matter-of-fact mechanistic attitude has some justification in the history of thought, but in the light of new quantum mechanics which thrives side by side with classical ways of thinking about space and movement, belonging to the time of the dawn of modern science with Newton and others, we have to be prepared for a revision of our ways of quantitative mechanistic thoughts in favour of live and pulsating vitalistic ones that can attain the core of problems that intimately concern the future of mankind as a whole. The horizontal way has to give place to the vertical.

The Whole and the Part in Normalized Reasoning

The dialectical is the path of higher wisdom which does not naturally fit with the light context of table-talk. The mechanistic is what the modern man of urban amenities living in London, Paris or New York adopts as a kind of substitute religion. Even a Sunday preacher, if he is to be popular, has to adapt himself to the spirit of the comic strips that the children pore over before coming to church with their quarters or dimes as the case may be. Serious talk is out of fashion and you stand the danger of being called an old fogey if you talk with any seriousness in company. The temper of modern civilization has to change if the impasse towards which civilization is heading is to be avoided.

The Dead End of Relativistic Law

Relativistic law is horizontal while its absolutist version is vertical. While I write these lines I am on a short visit to Varkala on the far southern end of the west coast of India, and although I do not look at newspapers regularly and was blissfully ignorant of the happenings in Assam over language, my eyes have been caught by headlines glanced at while travelling in trains. The most striking one was recently in which the president of a democracy and a chief minister dismissed each other. Both are right and both are wrong is the resulting absurdity. Even the possibility of such an event points to the blind alley towards which law and order seems to be heading. One side or the other may be held by those versed in mechanistic or horizontal aspects of law, but the monstrous absurdity can be solved only in the light of absolutist dialectics which is vertical. A Security Council, however powerful to intercede, would only add to the chaos, if the dialectical approach is unknown to its members. The diplomatic score might favour a "K" rather than an "I" here, the former being familiar with dialectical and not merely with the mechanistic. The truth implied is vital to the future of humanity.

Small Nations Must Live and Let Live

Coexistence, collective security, and political slogans such as One for All and All for One on which the Swiss Federation is based, are dialectical and not merely logical in content. The problem of minority groups like the Todas or Nagas in India and the Hopi Indians in America calls for a special kind of statesmanship which only the dialectical approach can yield. Partial and piecemeal unilateral solutions are sure to spell disaster. Instead of significant surds, the answers will be absurd disaster. Double gain or double loss has to be expected, and lukewarm half-hearted remedies are worse than none. The simple question of helping the Todas to live their lives *for, in* and *through* their own inner sense of values, seems a small one; but one who understands this on a small scale can alone be considered competent with the mass production of benefits for humanity in respect of any section, big or small thereof.

If we could think of a unit civilization, nation, culture or religion as a monad, there should be also a normative notion for it in a sort of Monad of monads in terms of a law for all humanity. Normative notions call for a science that is still to be formulated.

Index